SMARTER BANK

Published under licence 2015 by Searching Finance Ltd.

ISBN: 978-1-907720-82-6

Typeset and designed by Deirdré Gyenes

Printed in USA by Searching Finance

SMARTER BANK

WHY MONEY MANAGEMENT IS MORE IMPORTANT THAN MONEY MOVEMENT TO BANKS AND CREDIT UNIONS

by Ron Shevlin

About the author

Ron Shevlin has been a management consultant and technology analyst for 30 years, working for firms like Aite Group, Forrester Research, and KPMG Nolan Norton. His research and consulting focuses on sales and marketing technologies, customer and marketing analytics, social media, customer experience and consumer behavior.

Ron was listed #2 on Bank Innovation's list of 30 Innovators to Watch: Key Executives Shaping the Banking Industry in 2014. His blog, Snarketing 2.0, was named the #1 blog for financial services marketers by The Financial Brand in 2013, and was listed among Radius' 25 Best Marketing Blogs of 2014.

He has a BA in Economics from SUNY Binghamton and an MBA from the University of Texas at Austin.

About Searching Finance

Searching Finance publishes books on economics, finance, politics and history. Visit *www.searchingfinance.com*

CONTENTS

FOREWORD

RON SHEVLIN is famous for his snarky sense of humor, as well as his well-researched, well-considered takes on banking and customer behavior. We've collaborated on a couple of projects in recent years, and I've always found Ron to be a stand-up guy. That might be, however, because with his sense of humor, he should be doing stand-up comedy.

That said, when Ron starts talking about research he gets very serious, and very analytical—very fast. He takes rigorous and robust research very seriously. At the same time, he can have you cracking a smile or flat out chuckling along with his tongue-in-cheek and irreverent take on the fintech space.

Ron and I met in 2010 at the launch of my first book BANK 2.0. I can't remember why Ron was there, but the fact that he was there in those early days (before fintech was sexy) is important. He's been thinking about this book for nearly five years now, and it shows in the finished product.

Ron starts out in his introduction telling us that "if you're looking for a book that has exhortations that 'banks that don't do this are dinosaurs and will be left behind and go out of business,' go find another book." He then puts forward a plausible framework of some of the key problems facing the industry. The book is focused on the US market specifically, but many of the principles apply to broader geographies.

The first section tackles one of the hottest issues with the US market: Are there too many banks? I won't tell you what

Ron concludes, but I can tell you for each topic like this he brings lots of research and opinions to the table, and, in his usual style, explains why a lot of the research that has been done is flat out wrong. Having said that, Chapter 1 frames the book very well with one single, no-holds barred statement: The prevailing business model in retail banking is no longer viable.

At the end of the first chapter we get hit with our first view of Ron's Monty Python trained sense of humor (as compared with his Grateful Dead taste in music), but we immediately get serious again.

In the subsequent chapters, the book tackles some of the most fundamental structural issues and problems facing the banking sector, the most significant problems being that banks haven't really changed their operating model and business assumptions in decades. Ron demonstrates this with well timed flashbacks and trips into history. In a world where customer behavior and expectations are so rapidly changing, it quickly becomes clear that competing on location, rate, product or feature simply won't cut it in the era that is being thrust upon banks.

Ron has a unique way of viewing the world. A great example of this is when he says that in the discussions about trust, one of the most serious breaches of trust is that banks don't trust their customers anymore—it really got me thinking that that is a fundamental problem when you are trying to recreate customer experience in a customer-friendly manner. If you start out assuming the customer is an idiot or untrustworthy, what sort of a relationship are you going to foster? Having said that, there is no getting away from the fact that when you look at the data, banks may never be trusted again.

At its core, Smarter Bank tells us all the reasons why banks are just insisting on being dumb today—they're making rookie mistakes in an increasingly digital world, and have a really hard time making the technical, structural, cultural and process changes required to build really compelling engagement and relationship platforms. Ron tackles the problem of engagement from both an ongoing relationship perspective, at the same time explaining why the branch of the future won't get the brand to where it needs to go. He does, however, say that he will go to bank branches for the holographic obelisks and to see women in bathing suits (you'll understand when you get to that part of the book).

I don't agree with everything that Ron says when it comes to Gen Y, behavioral shifts, and some of the key drivers, but that's OK, because it is clear that Ron is putting forward hypotheses and he's up for debate on the nuances. One thing that I strongly agree with, though, is his conclusion that it is time we killed the underbanked. Not literally, of course, but that classification is doing more harm than good. The myth of financial literacy getting people to a level of product and financial talk sophistication so that they can 'graduate' to the formal banking system, is simply nonsense, and Ron calls it as it is. More importantly, he shows that the smarter bank knows how to provide a platform that no longer requires financial education or financial literacy to be of lasting benefit to its customers.

Smarter Bank is a smart book. If you are in banking, you should read it, and you will definitely come away smarter and better informed. At the end of the day, however, I think Ron proves convincingly that banks that don't follow his advice are dinosaurs and will definitely be left behind, and will most probably go out of business.

Thanks for your contribution, Ron.

Brett King
Author of *Breaking Banks* and Founder of Moven
www.brettking.com

Dedicated to my wife and three daughters.

INTRODUCTION

If you're reading this, it's likely that you're either a banker, credit union employee, work in the fintech industry, consult to banks and other financial institutions, or you're a journalist covering financial services. If this doesn't describe you, then you must be related to me.

The goal of this book is simple: Provide advice to the banking industry on how to get back on track to being a respectable industry, how to become more profitable, and how to deal with the technological disruptions that have emerged. As I write this, the industry is actually fairly profitable. But respectable? Not quite. Profitable and respectable need not be mutually exclusive.

In short, it's about how to become a "smarter" bank. Smarter in developing customer trust and relationships, smarter at understanding consumers' needs and wants, smarter at using technology, smarter at how to market products and services—and smarter about profits and revenue.

If you're looking for a book that has lots of examples of the cool things some banks are doing with technology, with exhortations that "banks that don't do this are dinosaurs and will be left behind and go out of business," go find another book.

This book is meant to take a critical look at trends and developments in the banking industry. You might not agree with all of "my takes." That's OK, neither do I. But I've got to argue one side of the coin to see if the rationale sticks.

Here's the flow of the book: Part One discusses the problems facing the banking industry, concluding that a new business model is needed in retail banking.

Part Two discusses three hurdles, or speed bumps, the industry must deal with in order to get a new model: Low consumer trust, low customer engagement, and dealing with all the bank branches that exist (and the costs they represent).

Part Three focuses on consumer trends, and discusses the behaviors and attitudes of various consumer segments.

Part Four highlights various technologies that may or may not impact the industry's ability to develop a new business model.

The last section, Part Five, discusses the organizational changes banks must deal with in order to successfully execute a new model.

Throughout the book, I've sprinkled "humor breaks" at the end of chapters to lighten up the mood. If I can't get you to agree with me on what the banking industry needs to become, at least maybe I can get you to smile along the way.

One note about terminology: Throughout the book, I use the term "banks" to refer to not just banks, but to credit unions, as well. Sorry, credit unions, I know that you're not banks. And I know that your members are members, not "customers." But when I refer, throughout the book, to bank customers, I'm also referring to credit union members.

Part I
Banking's Biggest Problem

Chapter One
What's the Problem in Banking?

Banking industry pundits like to point to the declining number of banks in the United States—from roughly 18,000 in the early 1980s to less than 7,000 in 2013—as a sign of the industry's decline.[1]

But a shrinking number of financial institutions isn't necessarily a sign of weakness, as deposits in banks have tripled over the past 30 years to nearly US$10 trillion. In fact, many industries demonstrate a pattern of consolidation, as acquirers seek to gain efficiencies of scale. There's no reason why the banking industry should be any different.

Matt Yglesias, writing in online magazine Slate, created a stir by essentially arguing that all community banks should be put to rest. Yglesias asserted that there are three basic problems with what he erroneously referred to as microbanks:[2]

"1. **They are poorly managed:** You know how the best and brightest of Wall Street royally screw up sometimes? This doesn't get better when you drill down to the less-bright and not-as-good guys. It gets worse. And since small banks finance themselves almost entirely with loans from Federal Deposit Insurance Corporation (FDIC)-ensured depositors, nobody is watching the store. In effect, the well-managed banks are being taxed to subsidize the poorly managed ones.

2. **They can't be regulated:** Since these banks are so small, they could be easily driven out of business by high regulatory compliance costs. So since American public policy is perversely committed to preserving them, small banks regularly get various kinds of carve-outs from regulations.

3. **They can't compete:** A bank serving a handful of rural counties or a single midsized city doesn't offer any real competition. Having a large share of America's banking sector tied up in tiny firms only makes it easier for a handful of big boys to monopolize big-time finance."

Unfortunately for Yglesias, there are no facts or data to support his claims. The Federalist refuted his arguments:[3]

"1. Compared to big banks (defined as those with more than a billion dollars in assets), small commercial banks (those with under $100 million in assets) have a higher ratio of equity-to-assets, a lower ratio of volatile liabilities-to-assets, a lower percentage of non-current loans and leases, and next to zero derivatives.

2. It wasn't local loans made and held by small community banks that caused the 2008 financial crisis. It was the big banks' hunger for risk, sated by an epic binge consisting of monstrously leveraged synthetic derivatives that caused the 2008 crisis.

3. According to the Independent Community Bankers of America, the federal government had, as of February of 2013, issued or proposed 900 new regulations since 2007. And if that source strikes you as a bit too biased, the Government Accountability Office wrote in a September 2012 study that regulations required by seven of Dodd-Frank's 16 titles would significantly affect community banks."

That still leaves us with one big question, however...

How Many Banks Do We Really Need?

In its description of the 1957 movie The Incredible Shrinking Man, Wikipedia states:[4]

"Robert Scott Carey is a businessman who is on vacation on a boat, off the Californian coast, when he suddenly is contaminated by a radioactive cloud. Six months later, Scott notices that his shirt seems too big. He blames it on the cleaners. His wedding ring falls off his finger. As this trend continues, Scott believes he is shrinking. Scott visits a research lab and learns that exposure to the radioactive mist caused his cells to shrink. He is told that he will never return to his former size, unless a cure is found, and that the antidote will only arrest the shrinking. The film's ending implies Scott will eventually shrink to atomic size; but, no matter how small he shrinks, Scott concludes he will still matter in the universe and this thought gives him comfort and ends his fears of the future."

Sounds like the banking industry, no? Shrinking, told it will never return to its former size, but comforted in believing that it still matters in the universe.

In *The Shrinking U.S. Banking Sector: On Balance, Who Benefits?*, Knowledge@Wharton makes some points about the consolidation of the banking industry that warrants a closer look.[5]

K@W: "We don't really need as many banks as we used to," says Jack Guttentag, a former economist at the Federal Reserve Bank of New York. "Banks now have the power to [set up branches] wherever they want to, so what really matters is how many options a customer has in a certain market."

My take: The options that customers have in any particular market is not determined by how many banks establish a branch (or branches) in that market. Consumers can open checking accounts, put money in a savings account, apply for loans, etc. with any number of providers, regardless of the provider's geographic location. Although the absolute number of financial institutions might be declining, thanks to the Internet, the effective number of providers that any one customer can do business with has increased.

K@W: A market, such as the one in the U.S., that is "over-banked," with a supply of banking services exceeding demand, is generally good for consumers because it results in lower prices—i.e., lower loan rates, loan/deposit fees and higher deposit rates—and higher output [in terms of] more varied and innovative products. Some may argue that 'over-competition' [or over-banking] could drive weaker banks out of business—as happened to Washington Mutual in 2008—but then someone else comes in and replaces them, yet may reduce the number of offices and amount of services.

My take: There are two points to respond to here. First, regarding the US as being "over-banked" because the "supply of services exceeds demand." What does that mean?

In a market of physical goods, it's possible for supply and demand to be out of alignment—that is, too much or too little supply relative to the demand. But banking products are virtual products. There is no physical supply. How can anyone determine that the supply exceeds demand?

Theoretically, the entire demand for all checking accounts in the US could be met by a single bank, if it had enough computing power to handle the load. The concept of service capacity in the world of banking is not analogous to the concept of manufacturing capacity in physical product industries.

Second, if you believe that over-competition drove Washington Mutual out of business, then you're smoking something still illegal in most states.

K@W: The institutions that will likely be hardest hit will be the community banks. For many of them, the arrival of the recent Dodd-Frank Wall Street Reform and Consumer Protection Act was a death knell. Tougher controls involving capital, liquidity and leverage, and a surge in regulatory red tape, have left such banks struggling, particularly those with less than $500 million of assets.

My take: Amen.

K@W: "Even if the number of banks shrinks from 6,000 to 100, if those 100 are operating in all market segments and if consumers have many options, there is no reason for concern," Guttentag says.

My take: This is a tricky statement. On one hand, there is some truth to it—if a customer truly has 100 providers to choose from, you'd have a tough time convincing anyone that this isn't sufficient choice.

But what concerns me is the part that says "if those 100 are operating in all market segments." For a bank to operate in all market segments, it would have to be pretty big. The largest banks in the U.S. don't have branches in every state. Do we really want 100 mega-banks in the industry?

When Guttentag refers to market segments, he's likely referring to geographic segments. But geography is irrelevant in a market for virtual products and services. Customer segments are far more relevant. The challenge, however, is that while geographies are—more or less—well defined, customer segments aren't. So it's very unlikely that 100 firms could possibly serve all segments.

The Real Reason That There May Be Too Many Banks

An American Banker editorial, *What Matthew Yglesias Should Have Said About Small Banks,* posited that the disparity of operating performance across smaller banks is the reason there are too many banks.[6] Well, at least, I think that's what the gist of the article is. According to the article:

> "There are currently over 900 publicly traded banks and thrifts with a market capitalization over $10 million. Twenty percent of those 900 or so institutions have returns on average tangible common equity (ATCE) over 12.3%. Five percent are over 17.2%. The bottom 30% post returns below 5.7%. Is 5.7% acceptable? Perhaps it doesn't look horrible in absolute terms in today's ultra-low interest rate environment, but it is horrible any way you cut it."

My take: The variability of average tangible common equity in 900 banks doesn't prove that 7,000 banks is too large a number.

There could be any number of reasons why a bank's ATCE is below 5.7%. And probably any number of ways that a bank could increase the ATCE to 17.2%. Should we just eliminate all banks with an ATCE below a certain level? Even if we should, at what level should the cutoff be? For how long should a bank be below that level before we kill it off? One performance metric is not a sign that there are too many banks.

There is, however, one argument to justify the claim that there are too many banks in the US: Supply outstrips demand.

If an industry's production capacity (i.e., supply) exceeds the long-term demand for its products and services, then there is excess capacity. Existing providers can: 1) Reduce production capacity; 2) Go out of business; or 3) Find a way to increase demand.

Over the past five years, the combination of a weak economy and the regulatory changes imposed by the government have depressed demand for financial services.

By demand, I'm referring to unit volume and total revenue. Consumer demand for mortgages and credit cards declined as a result of the recession. But the overall level of revenue generated by banks has also been suppressed by the pricing limitations (on credit card interest, on overdraft fees, etc.) imposed by regulations.

If the reduced level of demand for financial services is systemic and persistent, then an argument can be made that there are too many banks (and credit unions).

But the number of banks and credit unions doesn't necessarily have to decrease, banks could shrink through layoffs and shedding unproductive assets. But if the aggregate demand—across financial products and services—is significantly lower than it was in the past, this would be a unsuccessful strategy, and the number of banks would have to decrease.

So that leaves us with option 3. Find a way to increase demand.

You might be inclined to argue that the demand for financial services/products is actually there, but not being adequately captured by banks. For example, you might argue that banks could increase "demand" by capturing the P2P (person-to-person) lending volume that's out there. But you'd be wrong, and you'd be misinterpreting the definition of supply and demand.

If I say I want a Maserati, does that constitute "demand" for a Maserati? There's no way I can afford a Maserati (well, maybe I could, but good luck getting my wife to spend all of our retirement savings). For Maserati to capture that "demand," it would have to lower the price of the car to point at which it wouldn't be profitable to them. So no, my interest isn't really demand.

This is analogous to banks and P2P lending. Banks have lending guidelines. The demand for loans constitutes the demand that fits those guidelines. One way of increasing demand for loans is to loosen the guidelines. Basically, credit card issuers have done that to increase demand for cards.

But as long as banks maintain lending guidelines—i.e., maintain profitable pricing levels—that exclude certain consumers, P2P borrowers won't constitute demand. In other words, P2P borrowing is demand for a different product or service than what banks provide.

If banks' attempts to increase market demand is limited to finding new ways to sell existing products and services, they're screwed unless: 1) the economy heats up, and/or 2) new generations produce significantly new numbers of customers.

If either of these things happen, it just proves that the current reduced level of demand is not systemic and persistent.

The other way that the existing number of banks can remain stable is if they develop new products and services to sell that grow the overall level of demand. The current track record among banks for doing just that isn't particularly good. Banks don't typically charge customers to use personal financial management (PFM) or online bill pay tools, and P2P payments has failed to generate much revenue.

The innovations that the market seems to get excited about—things like Coin, Loop, or other mobile payment-related stuff—don't generate additional demand for banks' products and services.

Mobile technologies aren't the cause of banks going out of business. It's the reduced level of demand for financial products and services. Mobile technologies have helped create alternative suppliers to meet the existing level of demand, but that's just one factor chipping away at the number of banks. In fact, mobile offers as much opportunity to banks to find ways to create new demand by leveraging the technology to create new products and services.

Bottom line: The real reason why there may be too many banks is the excess of supply over demand.

What's The Real Problem Facing Banks?

Some observers believe that keeping up with and adapting to technological innovations—and the consumer behaviors that change, as a result—is a problem banks wrestle with. But banks have a good track record of adapting to, and implementing new technologies. Witness, for example, ATMs, online banking, online bill pay, eStatements, and remote deposit capture.

Consumer behaviors and attitudes are in constant flux in response to technological and societal changes. Consumers now use the Internet to do practically everything, and are increasingly using smartphones and tablets (which I'll refer to here as simply "mobile devices") to help with every aspect of their lives.

Technology innovation and change in banking has not led to a transformation of the industry, however. Instead, consumers have new points of contact, or channels, to interact with banks. And banks have new channels to improve service delivery and reduce costs.

The problem here—if there is one—is how to balance and prioritize investments in the development and enhancement of capabilities in all these channels. This is a challenge for banks, for sure, but not the biggest problem they face.

No, changing consumer behaviors and technologies aren't banks' biggest problems (in fact, they're solutions to the real problem).

What's the real problem facing retail banking?

My take: The prevailing business model in banking is no longer viable.

The Death Of The Traditional Business Model

The prevailing business model in retail banking is a balancing act between debit and credit: Banks offer debit products (like checking and savings accounts) that enable them to acquire funds which they use to provide loans to people (and businesses) that need them.

Revenue from interest-generating products (e.g., loans) comprise the vast majority. The demand for loans is cyclical, so short-term weakness in lending-related income shouldn't portend the death of the business model. But a number of trends indicates a business model problem:

1) **Decline in the percentage of interest-earning assets.** Since 1985, total assets held by U.S. banks increased from nearly US$2.3 trillion to more than US$13 trillion in 2013. Interest-earning assets, however, declined from nearly 13% of total assets to less than 10%. After growing 8% per year 2000 to 2010, interest-earning assets has declined by 1% annually since 2010.

2) **Decline in net interest margin.** As interest-earning assets flatten, the revenue banks make on them shrinks. Net interest margin—the difference between the interest income generated by banks and the amount of interest paid out to their lenders—reached a high of nearly 5% in 1995, and has trended downward since then, hitting a low of 3.15% at the depth of the recession in the third quarter of 2008. It rose back up to 3.7% in Q3 2010, retracted back to 3.2% by July 2013. With nearly US$1.2 trillion in interest-earning assets in the system, the decline between Q2 2010 and Q2 2013 reflects nearly US$5 billion in lost interest margin.

3) **Decline in overdraft income.** Between 1992 and 2009, revenue generated from overdraft fees grew from about US$11.3 billion to US$38.5 billion. With the introduction of regulations limiting banks' ability to levy these fees in 2009, overdraft fees declined to US$31.3 billion in 2013, a 19% drop from the peak. The combination of regulations and consumer anger with these fees will make it difficult, if not impossible, for banks to recoup this revenue.

4) **Decline in return on equity.** From about 1993 through 2007, industry return on equity (ROE) fluctuated in a narrow band of about 14% to 16%, before falling off the cliff in 2008. Since the depths of the recession, ROE has rebounded as profits have grown, but ROE has struggled

to break 10%. McKinsey estimates that industry profits could reach $154 billion by 2015, up 27% from its 2010 level. But for the industry to even reach 12% ROE in 2015, profits would have to nearly double to roughly $312 billion.[7]

Can the industry reverse these trends, and return to historic levels of profitability? Boston Consulting Group (BCG) believes that the industry can reach historical levels of ROE through: 1) Cost reduction, which could put three to four percentage points on the industry's ROE; 2) Price optimization, which could contribute one to two percentage points; and 3) Growth, which could add another point or two.[8]

Achieving BCG's estimates—with the current business model—will be a nearly impossible task for the industry. Why?

1) **Cost reduction opportunities are limited.** Two of the largest line items in banks' cost structure are branch-related costs, and check processing costs. Both line items have a large fixed cost component to them. Although many banks are closing branches, many that have done so are adding branches, as well. And not a single bank that I have found is eliminating its branch network altogether.

   In addition, although check volume has declined significantly in the past 10 years, the variable cost to process checks is relatively small, and the fixed component high. So, as check volume has diminished, banks' ability to rip out the check processing infrastructure—and the associated costs—has been limited.

   Conventional wisdom among bankers also limits cost reduction through branch closing. Despite the adoption of the Internet (and now mobile devices) to research financial products, the percentage of new account openings that occur in bank branches remains high. Many bankers believe that their institutions would lose that business if they didn't have their existing branch network.

2) **Pricing flexibility has been limited.** Regulatory efforts over the past few years in the United States has curtailed banks' ability to optimize prices. One regulation, referred to as Reg E, limited banks' ability to raise interest rates on credit cards. Another regulation changed the way banks could impose overdraft fees on checking accounts, resulting in a decline in NSF fees. The Durbin Amendment drastically cut the interchange rate banks earned on debit card transactions. And when many banks introduced monthly fees on what were previously free checking accounts, many customers fled to other institutions.

3) **Demographic changes will have a deleterious effect on the industry's long-term growth potential.** Within the confines of the existing business model, organic growth may be banks' best bet to improve industry return on equity (ROE). Remember, however, that the current business model is dependent upon demand for credit. While it remains to be seen if Gen Yers' current attitudes will persist, this generation has demonstrated a distaste for credit card debt, has said that owning a car is not an absolute must for them, and may be resigned to living in a society where home ownership is not the end-all and be-all it was to previous generations.

All three of the factors will dampen demand for financial products and services, making organic growth difficult.

Bottom line: Returning to the historical level of ROE in banking is improbable, if not impossible, within the confines of the prevailing business model. The prevailing model is dead.

Humor Break
Bank Mergers I'd Like to See

Capital One +BofA +Fifth Third =
ONE FIFTH OF A THIRD

Capital One + Huntington Bancshares + People's Bank =
HUNTING POPULAR PEOPLE

Union Bank of California + Aegon = Calgon

North Fork +ING = No Forking

Synovus + Citigroup = SynCiti

Dollar Bank + UMB Financial = DUMB

Schwab + Raymond James + UBS = SCRUBS

Don't hold your breath waiting for these mergers.

Chapter Two
The Innovation Question

An American Banker article claimed that financial firms are "behind in innovation," and quoted a Boston Consulting Group (BCG) exec, who said that the financial services industry "could do even better if it raised the bar on innovation. Financial services execs shouldn't take their foot off the gas when it comes to innovation; they should accelerate."

Really? Do you know of FIs that consciously say "We need to slow down here—we're innovating way too much, way too fast"? I don't. The problem isn't that financial firms are decelerating, or even considering slowing down their rate of innovation. The issue is threefold: 1) Defining innovation; 2) Dealing with politics; and 3) Establishing business priorities.

A BCG study found that "only" 53% of FIs said innovation is a priority (versus 67% of those from other industries). What BCG didn't say, however, was how did the survey respondents define innovation?

My hunch is that many survey respondents equated innovation with disruptive, strategic change. And—if I'm right—therein lies the problem: Confusing "big I" innovation (large scale, disruptive innovations) with "little I" innovation (feature or functionality improvements).

Introducing revolutionary new products and services is rare to the world of retail financial services. But feature and function improvements—or innovations—are introduced all the time. It would be interesting to know if many within the financial services industry consider this innovation.

The second innovation challenge that banks face is political.

The BCG study found that "part of the problem in financial services is lack of support among top executives." James Gardner, the former Head of Innovation and Research at Lloyds TSB, understands this well. As he wrote on his blog, some members of his firm are hesitant about the results his group will be able to achieve because:

> "They wonder how we will ever get the support of the business to fund any of our initiatives, given that budgets are fixed, and other business-as-usual projects always take precedence."

Addressing the first issue (definition) and overcoming the second (politics) can only be accomplished by taking care of the third challenge: Strategy.

Gardner said in his blog that Lloyds TSB will go from 1,500 ideas to 64 business cases, to 30 pilots, of which 7 or 8 will "see the market and/or go live". What he doesn't mention (and I don't want to imply that he doesn't have this nailed down) is what the prioritization process looks like. Lloyds might have this down to a science—if it does, it's in a small, elite group of financial firms.

This is the biggest challenge financial firms (and banks in particular) have when it comes to innovation. They're not sure where to focus. Capital One recently introduced a new product innovation. Should other large firms follow? Or would service or process innovations better suit their strategies?

Who knows, because few of them have clear, well articulated, well understood strategies to guide their innovation decisions.

No one I know of in the financial services world is taking their "foot off the gas pedal." But there are some challenges that must be addressed before the innovation engine can be revved up.

Innovation Snobs

Let's get a couple of things straight, right from the top: 1) I'm not against innovation, and 2) I apologize in advance to anyone who is offended by the title of this section, thinking that I'm referring specifically to them. It's just that I don't see it as the cure for and salvation to everything. And, sorry, but there are some innovation "snobs" out there.

These innovation snobs continually harp on: 1) How firms need to "innovate" their way out of just about any problem or situation they get into, and 2) How firms that don't "innovate" are somehow missing the boat, or doomed to fail. Sadly, innovation snobs often fail to understand a couple of things.

First, is the difference between product and organizational innovation. This difference is spelled out very well in a white-paper from Harvard Business School professor Gary Pisano called The Evolution of Science-Based Business: Innovating How We Innovate. The paper states:[9]

> "Alfred Chandler taught us that organizational innovation and technological innovation are equal partners in the process of economic growth. Indeed, one often requires the other. Today, the technologies driving growth are, of course, quite different than they were a century ago. But, the fundamental lesson—that these technologies may require new organizational forms—is as relevant today as it was then."

Maybe it's just my perception, but it does seem to me that the innovation snobs continually beat the drums for technology innovation, and fail to pay attention to the organizational side of the coin.

This is especially true in the world of banking, where the list of technology innovations over the past 20 to 30 years is quite impressive: ATMs, online banking, online bill pay, remote deposit capture, mobile banking, PFM, debit card, prepaid cards. The list goes on.

Yet banks have been slow to innovate organizationally. Product- and channel-centric departments still dominate. Most banks can't calculate a reliable customer profitability number. And marketing ROI measurement remains a black art.

I had a recent conversation with a senior exec at a credit union who, for the record, is not an innovation snob. He recently saw Hal Varian of Google present some really cool ideas about how organizations could radically change the way they do things using data from Google.

My friend asked me if I thought some of the ideas were applicable to financial services. My immediate thought was: "Hell yes! This is amazing stuff!" followed by "but, most financial services firms can't even integrate their own Web data with their offline data, can't figure out how to use behavioral and not just demographic data to make marketing decisions, can't look past their own data to make pricing and risk decisions, etc. — How the hell are they going to incorporate Google's data?"

The second thing the innovation snobs fail to realize is that imitation isn't inherently bad. Oded Shenkar, a professor at Ohio State University, found imitation to be a "primary source of progress, even though that progress often went unrecognized by executives and scholars."[10]

The point is that if firms only did things that reflected their own innovations, there are a lot of things we'd be missing out on. Just remember, all my little Apple fanboy friends, that Apple did not create the graphical user interface. That came from Xerox. I don't hear the innovation snobs taking Apple to task for this, though.

But hey, I guess there's a market for innovation snobbery, primarily in the form of blog posts for innovation snobs to reinforce each other's view of innovation as marketplace savior. And who am I to criticize someone for meeting the demand for something that's out there.

Maybe Banks Don't Have To Innovate

Rather than arguing whether or not the assertion that banks haven't innovated is true, let's assume for a moment that it is. The key question, then, is: Why don't banks innovate (or why haven't banks innovated)?

Is it: a) They're too stupid to innovate; b) They don't know how to innovate; c) They're too risk averse to innovate; or d) There's been no need to innovate?

If I were to take a poll, I'd bet that the majority of respondents would answer B, followed by C—even though many of you would like to select A. I think the answer is D.

When the Innovation Snobs talk about innovation what they're really looking for is large-scale change in the industry. After all, there have been plenty of technology "innovations" in the industry like ATMs, online banking, online bill pay, PFM, mobile banking, remote deposit capture, etc., but none of these developments satisfy the snobs.

Despite these innovations, the industry has changed little in terms of power structure and business model (as it applies to the retail sector, that is). Why haven't we seen large-scale, transformational change—or innovation—in the industry, despite the advent of the Internet, the Web, and more recently, mobile technologies?

Because—until recently—there has been no need for the industry to change. For large scale change to happen in retail banking, three elements need to be in place: technology change, demographic change, and economic imperative. There's no formula, but if one of these elements isn't sufficiently present, change isn't going to happen.

Since the mid-90s, the emergence of Internet technologies has created the technology change required to cause industry innovation or transformation. With the advent of mobile technologies, even more technological change is pushing the industry to change.

Many Innovation Snobs think that this is sufficient to cause change, but it isn't. And one reason why the technology change wasn't enough was because we didn't have sufficient demographic change.

Ten, even five, years ago, Boomers and Seniors dominated the generational composition of the US population. While we were willing to try technologies like online banking and bill pay, and even willing to open online savings accounts with a firm like ING Direct, we still did our banking business the old-fashioned way: We opened up checking accounts with the same old providers we did 20 or 30 years ago (although many of them merged along the way, of course).

It's only been more recently that the demographic shifts required to effect industry change have come about. The emergence of Gen Yers as a significant percentage of the US population is a recent phenomenon. What's different about this generation (from a financial services perspective) is their willingness (or desire) to find an alternative to checking accounts. When Seniors, Boomers, and even Gen Xers became adults, we automatically opened up a checking account. Not so with Gen Yers.

Without this demographic shift, the simple development of online banking, bill pay, etc. was insufficient to bring about large-scale industry change.

But even the demographic shift by itself isn't—and hasn't—been enough. There's another reason why innovation hasn't occurred, and I think the Innovation Snobs really miss this point: There has been (until recently) no economic imperative to change.

Ten years ago I did some consumer research about the drivers of customer loyalty in banking. I went out to my bank clients to tell them the findings, and tell them what they had to do differently to improve customer loyalty. Their response was pretty underwhelming: "Why should we do anything differently when we're making money hand over fist?"

They had a point. As we discussed in the previous chapter, from about 1993 through 2007, bank industry ROE fluctuated in a narrow band of about 13% to 15%, before falling off the cliff in 2008. With those kinds of returns, who's got an incentive to change?

This is why we haven't seen the innovation that the snobs have called for. The elements of change haven't sufficiently been in place. With the advent of mobile technologies, the shift in demographics, and the economic issues facing the industry, we are finally on the cusp of change.

Banks' Innovation Imperative

Will the impending changes render banks obsolete, and cause them to disappear like the dinosaurs? Some pundits would obviously like that, but it's not going to happen. One academic study found that:[11]

> "Disruptive innovations need not lead to an incumbent's fall, despite prevailing academic theory arguing otherwise. Startups introducing disruptive technologies are more likely to end up licensing to incumbents or agreeing to be acquired rather than turning into rivals. Once the technology is proven, among other factors, start-ups tend to form alliances or merge with market leaders, thus preserving the status quo."

The authors of the study call a startup's switch from competition to cooperation with incumbents a "dynamic technology commercialization strategy." The rest of us call it "selling out" (that was a joke).

My take: Although the authors of the study based their conclusions on an analysis of the automatic speech recognition industry, many of their findings apply to banking.

What does the research (cited above) say about the Chicken Little pronouncements that banks must "adapt or die" or that they will be "Kodaked"? It says that what banks really need to be able to do is: 1) Monitor and assess technological innovations' market potential; 2) Acquire (i.e., invest in) those innovations at the right time; and 3) Deploy (i.e., assimilate or exploit) the acquired innovations.

Now, you might say that this capability is an "innovation" (i.e., process innovation) in and of itself, but c'mon–you have to admit that what most Chicken Littles refer to when they say "innovation" is technology innovation.

So, maybe banks don't have to innovate.

But they're not off the hook. Of the three steps above, #2 is hard and #3 is really difficult. I don't mean to imply that #1 is easy–but there are firms out there (like the one I work for, or Bank Innovators Council) who can help with it.

Determining the right time to acquire a particular innovation depends on a number of factors, many of which will be hotly contested by various factions within the bank.

One of the more controversial calls I made as an analyst came about in the early 2000s when I told banks to not investing in mobile banking at the time. My argument was that there were higher priorities that deserved investment.

I had a colleague at the time who wrote the opposite.

The chief technology officer of a very large bank flew both of us down to his office to make our case to him and his team. I won the debate, and the bank chose not to allocate funds to mobile banking in the coming year. About a year later, I got an email from him saying it was the right call, and that I helped him put about $5 million towards things that really needed to be developed/fixed (I actually got an email from the SVP, of eCommerce at another large bank with the same story and thanks).

CHAPTER THREE
THE NEW COMPETITIVE DYNAMIC

Since 1950, the banking industry has progressed through two phases of competitive dynamics. The first competitive dynamic, which was predominant until the mid-1980s, was competing on location. The bank with the most bank branches, in the most desirable locations, staffed by the most helpful personnel, gained deposits and won customers' checking account business.

The next dynamic, gaining force in the mid-1980s and predominant through 2011, was competing on rates, as banks stressed their superior rates and fees. The third dynamic, just emerging now, is competing on performance—the banks that help their customers best manage their financial lives (and quantifies that performance) will win.

A new competitive dynamic is emerging—and with it a new prevailing business model—based on improving consumers' personal financial performance.

Competing on Location

The number of bank branches in the United States grew from roughly 1,000 in 1940 to nearly 84,000 in 2012. The number of branches per capital grew steadily from the 1960s through to 2012, from about 10 branches per 100,000 people in 1968 to nearly 20 branches per 100k people in 1988, peaking at 27 branches in 2012.

Branch location has long been cited as the primary factor influencing consumers' choice of banks. Even today, with the prevalence of online-only, and now mobile-centric, banks, consumers still point to branch location as the determining factor in deciding who to bank with. According to a Mintel study from October 2012, half of US consumers said that they chose their bank because of a branch near their home—a significantly higher proportion than any other reason listed. And nine in 10 said that it was important to them to have a bank branch nearby.

In fact, according to a survey from FindABetterBank.com, an online bank comparison site, 53% of Americans wouldn't consider an institution without a branch nearby, and 29% can't imagine a time in the future when they would be comfortable doing all their banking virtually.

It's a safe bet, however, that 50 years ago, nearly *all* Americans wouldn't consider an institution without a branch nearby and couldn't imagine banking "virtually," because that concept didn't exist then.

Even if the concept existed, it wouldn't have mattered. Our financial lives were much simpler back then. The role of the bank was primarily one of "store and pay." People cashed their paychecks, deposited some of it in a checking account, and wrote checks to pay bills and buy goods.

Bank ads, like the one shown below from Bank of America from 1954, stressed the local nature of the bank and its community involvement (Figure 3.1). In fact, the bankers of the 1950s were so friendly, one bank emphasized in its ads how its CEO never foreclosed on a mortgage (Figure 3.2)!

Figure 3.1

Figure 3.2

Even if the Internet had been around from 1945 to 1965, it's unlikely to have had much impact on the competitive dynamics of banking. Americans' disposable income and demand for credit grew slowly in this period. But starting in the 1960s, through to the second decade of the 21st century, personal income and demand for credit in the United States skyrocketed (Figure 3.3 and Figure 3.4).

Figure 3.3

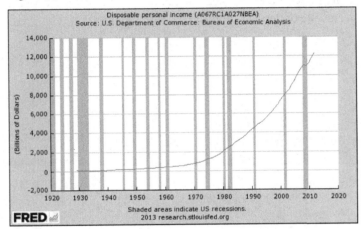

Source: FDIC

Figure 3.4

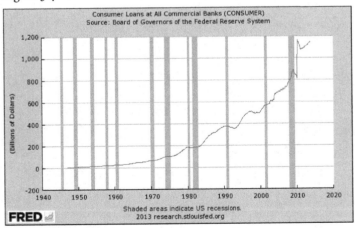

Source: FDIC

The increase in personal income created demand for deposit and credit, and created a new competitive dynamic in banking: Competing on rates and fees. This new basis of competition changed the nature of advertising, as well. Typical of the era was the Wells Fargo ad below, which emphasized no minimum balance, no service charge, travelers checks for no service charge, 5% interest on deposits, and 7.5% interest on a 6-year certificate of deposit (Figure 3.5). Sign me up!

Figure 3.5

Source: http://www.vintageadbrowser.com/money-ads-1970s/23

The focus on rates and fees wasn't limited to checking accounts. In this 1976 ad, Manufacturers Hanover (now part of…oh, never mind, who can keep track of all the bank mergers?) exhorts car shoppers to shop for the best rate on their car loan, as well as looking for the best deal on the car itself (Figure 3.6).

Figure 3.6

Source: http://www.vintageadbrowser.com/money-ads-1970s/6

Location took on a new meaning in this second competitive dynamic, shifting from a focus on friendly, local service to the convenience of multiple locations. The emergence of ATMs in the mid-70s meant consumers were no longer limited to banking when the branches were open, and many banks emphasized this convenience in their marketing efforts, including this 1976 ad from MidLantic Bank (Figure 3.7).

The rates-and-fees dynamic did not replace the location dynamic. The two co-existed as banks competed on both dimensions, despite their often-claimed unwillingness to compete on rates and fees.

These seemingly incompatible competitive dimensions coexisted because of consumer behavior. On one hand, with increased levels of education among Americans (in 1940 just 25% of Americans had completed four years of high school or more, by 1975, that percentage had reached 65%), consumers wanted to believe that they were making a rational decision on who to do business with.

In this case, rational meant economic—i.e., who had the best rates and fees. Helpful, friendly service, local knowledge, and community support were non-rational (i.e., immeasurable) factors that consumers don't like to admit to being influencers in their decisions.

Figure 3.7

Performance: The New Competitive Dynamic

Bank customers have learned some hard lessons about banking over the past 25 years. One of those lessons is that free doesn't mean free (at least when it comes to checking accounts).

A so-called "free" checking account is one that doesn't charge a monthly fee. But these accounts still charge for overdraws, out-of-network ATM use, and a host of other things. The lure of free checking didn't mean that at the end of the year, a customer didn't spend up to hundreds of dollars to keep that checking account open.

Another lesson consumers learned was that a lower interest rate on one loan than another might make that first loan seem like the better deal, but when you consider points and fees on the loan, the second loan might turn out to be the better proposition.

A third lesson: That the rewards earned on many credit cards, and more recently, on checking accounts, might not be as attractive as they sound if the points are never redeemed. Or if, in the case of credit cards, interest payments made on the card wipe out the dollar value of the rewards earned.

An even more painful lesson: The great return on that mutual fund isn't so great if the management costs for the fund are high. In other words, that return on the investment you thought you got wasn't the ROI you really got.

It didn't used to matter that much. Before 1980, most Americans weren't investors. They had savings accounts and relied on pensions for their retirement years.

The introduction of financial products like 401(k) plans, certificates of deposit, and 529 plans, coupled with the easy availability of credit in the form of mortgages, home equity loans, credit cards, and payday loans contributed to the complexity of the average American's financial life.

What's missing? Someone to tell us how we're doing.

Total Benefits of Ownership

IT professionals have a concept called total cost of ownership (TCO). The idea is that the price tag on a piece of software or hardware is only one aspect of what it really costs to own that asset. Other costs include implementation and customization expenses, as well as ongoing maintenance and enhancement costs.

Consumers need a similar concept. Not tracking the total cost of owning financial services and products, but the total (or net) benefit of having all those accounts.

The PFM tools available from banks (and from websites like Mint.com) aren't the answer. PFM has become too narrowly linked to budgeting and expense categorization. Nice features, but not what a lot of people want. Performance isn't just about getting the best savings rate or lowest mortgage rate. It's about helping customers save more, getting the best deals on what they buy, about choosing the right way to pay for the things they purchase, and about avoiding fees. And charging them for those capabilities.

While consumer advocate groups will point out the so-called hidden costs of financial services (they're not really hidden if you take the time to read the schedule of fees that are available on just about any bank's website), there are benefits that are untracked and not accounted for.

Bank of America runs a program for its customers called Museums On Us. It gives BofA customers free admission to a number of museums around the country on the first weekend of every month.

When my wife and I took advantage of this program a few months ago, we got into the Museum of Fine Arts in Boston for free. At $25 per admission, we save $50. But this savings doesn't show up on our monthly statement from the bank.

While banks and credit card issuers have long shown rewards cardholders the points they've accumulated and redeemed, they've never tracked the actual savings the customers have realized from these rewards.

These benefits should be weighed against the costs of keeping these accounts and cards open, no? But the tracking of benefits and costs doesn't happen today because banks can't calculate an ROI on making the investment to track all the benefits and costs.

Banks will compete in the future by how well they help their customers manage their financial lives, maximizing the benefits-to-cost ratio associated with their financial accounts and products.

The Value Perception Challenge

To a large extent, the new, emerging competitive dynamic is about quantifying and proving the value being delivered to the customer. One reason why this has become an imperative is that public sentiment is going against the banks.

The Washington Post published an editorial titled *What Are You Worth To Your Bank?* presenting a model for how much a bank makes off a customer.[12]

The model estimated a customer's worth to a bank is equal to the fees the customer pays plus 2.5% of what's in checking/savings accounts plus 1.75% of that customer's card-based (credit and/or debit) transactions.

It made assumptions about average income levels ($60k per year), spending and savings patterns ($10k in checking/savings, $12k spending per year), conservatively assumed that a customer can avoid fees, and put the average customer value at around $500.

My take: The assumptions of the model are reasonable, but it ignored the cost side of the equation, so it really doesn't estimate the "value" of a customer to a bank, but simply the revenue generated. The editorial posed the following questions:

"Do you feel you get half a grand worth of service from your bank? Or are they difficult to deal with for customer service, pushy and abrasive when it comes to trying to get you to take on new products? Half a grand might be what you pay for a basic cable service; do you get that much quality from your bank?"

What about the financial benefits that a customer might accrue? Using the model's checking, savings, and spending figures, let's assume that:

1. A customer puts $10k in a high-yield account and earns 2.5% interest, or $250 (for simplicity's sake let's not get into the compounding).

2. The customer has a rewards-based debit and credit card, and gets 1% cash back on her spending. The cash back on the $12k of spending comes to $120.

3. The customer uses online bill pay, and saves US$5 per month on postage costs.

Result: The bank makes $500 off the customer, but the "value" to the customer totals $435.

Few—if any—banks monitor, track, and report to its customers the "value" they provide. This is why the industry needs a new competitive dynamic.

The FinScore: The Missing Ingredient

Exactly how well is someone doing regarding his or her financial life? And how does that financial performance compare to everyone else? We can't answer these questions because there is no universally-accepted score (think of it as a FinScore) that measures this.

One of the distinguishing financial services-related characteristics of Gen Yers is their awareness and understanding of the concept of the credit score. Baby boomers didn't know what a credit score was, let alone what their own score was, when they were in their 20s (OK, that wasn't really fair, since the FICO score wasn't introduced until 1989 when most Boomers were already in their 30s).

It wasn't until recently that Americans truly became aware of what a credit score was, and how it impacted the interest rate they got on their credit cards and loans. Services like Credit Karma have emerged to help consumers track their credit score, and understand how their financial-related actions impact their credit score.

But the credit score is a tool that financial institutions use to rate consumers' creditworthiness. From a consumer perspective, it's not a useful financial management or measurement tool.

Based on their financial behaviors, my in-laws probably have a lousy credit score. And I doubt they could care less. Getting credit from a financial institution isn't something they're too worried about getting. Yet, you and I should be so lucky to be in as good a financial situation as they are.

Exactly how well are they doing? And how much "better" are they doing, financially, than you or I?

Americans love to grade and score things. We brag about our SAT score, our college GPA, our Klout score, even our cholesterol score. We love to know how we're doing, and how we're doing relative to everyone else.

How much money we make (annual income) has historically been the metric of how well we're doing financially, but if you have a $500k mortgage and three kids between the ages of 10 and 20, you're not doing as well as someone making the same amount who has no kids and no mortgage on the identical house to the one you own. Or maybe based on other factors and behaviors, you are. Who knows?

So we need a FinScore. A single number that tells us how we're doing. There are some firms working on this. Moven has its CRED score, and a startup called FlexScore has its eponymous score.

Based on a consumer's financial assets, liabilities, behaviors, and demographics—among other factor—FlexScore determines a score between a range of 0 and 800 (Figure 3.8).

Figure 3.8

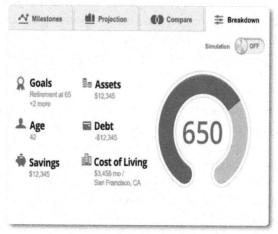

Source: FlexScore

In addition, actions and activities—like setting up recurring deposits, or paying off debts—impact that score by a certain amount (Figure 3.9).

Figure 3.9

Source: FlexScore

Practically speaking, though, no matter how good (i.e., accurate) the CRED or FlexScore is, the challenge for the two startups—and any other firm that wants to create a score—is driving broad (if not ubiquitous) adoption.

An established, more widely known financial institution may try to develop its own score, but that effort is likely to run into the "what's the ROI of this initiative?" mentality that kills plenty of potentially good ideas at banks

Although I don't see any existing banks working on developing this score, it's in the best interest of banks and credit unions to see a widely-accepted FinScore emerge. Here's why: The next wave of banking competition is competing on performance. That is, who best helps the customer manage and improve their financial lives—and not who has the best rates or fees, or who claims to have the best service.

With a universally accepted FinScore, consumers will be able to make educated decisions about who to bank with based on: 1) How important improving their FinScore is to them, 2) Which financial institution promises to best improve that FinScore—and ultimately delivers on that promise, and 3) The cost to the consumer for getting an X-point improvement in their FinScore.

Banks will brag that they helped their customers average a 25-point improvement in their FinScore over the past year, and that their competitors' customers didn't do as well.

Competing on performance is the future of retail banking— but the industry needs a FinScore to make it happen.

The New Business Model in Banking

In his book, *Bank 3.0*, Brett King wrote:[13]

"The bank account is becoming unhinged from the bank. Once we can pay with our phone, and it is connected to a value store—this is a far better banking utility than a basic current/checking account. A bank still issuing cheque books simply doesn't provide a competitive platform to compete with a mobile wallet, and businesses don't need a banking license to power a value store on a wallet."

I agree with the spirit of what King is saying, but not as it's written. The second sentence should say "A bank that *only issues* cheque books doesn't provide a competitive platform..."

The challenge banks face isn't in the issuance of a check book (or checking account). It's the lack of value that consumers get from only being able to make payments with the account.

The rebanking (reinvention, redesign) of the industry rests on banks' ability to change a belief that generations of bankers have held: That the core purpose of banking is to move money.

The rebanking of the industry rests on banks' ability to change the core purpose from *moving* money to *managing* money.

You might think that this is what financial advisors have been doing for years. Nope. They've typically focused on helping a small percentage of people maximize the performance of their financial assets. But the mass market doesn't need help allocating assets (investments), they need help in managing liabilities (expenses).

There's no money for advisors in doing that. And banks haven't been able to do it. As long as people paid in cash or checks, (or with credit cards that weren't issued by the bank), banks have been hampered by a business model that offers no reward for providing advice and guidance in managing day-to-day expenditures.

To re-bank the industry, banks must find and create new ways to add value to their customers that go beyond—way beyond—simply being able to write a check or use a debit (or credit) card.

If consumers see value in these new products, services, and features, then they will gladly pay for it (OK, maybe not gladly, but, at the least, without the threats of lawsuits that accompany every new fee or rate hike that is announced today).

The new business model in retail banking will be driven by revenues that don't just rely on big-ticket items like mortgages, car loans, and overdraft fees.

The new retail bank will become a hub for its customers' financial services needs. Connecting customers with a wide range of providers of services—like credit score monitoring, credit card grey charge tracking, rewards management, savings incentives, spend optimization, monthly bill management, and more—who can't economically reach a wide range of consumers on their own, and who need the bank's help to integrate their services into a cohesive and coherent offering.

In this new model, banks generate revenue not just from consumers, but from service providers, as well as from retailers and merchants, based on the banks' ability to reach and sell into their customer base.

This means that banks will have to become good B2B (business-to-business) marketers as well as B2C (business-to-consumer) marketers. Although, banks' competency in B2C marketing is suspect, as it is.

In the emerging business model of retail banking, banks may make as much money selling other firms' products and services as they do from selling their own.

Banks Can't Compete on Service

The underlying premise of this book is that banks will have to compete, in the future, on performance (their customers' personal financial performance).

Many people won't agree with me, believing, instead, that banks can, and will, compete on superior customer service. According to social media celebrity Gary Vaynerchuk, "any business can create a competitive advantage through giving outstanding customer care:"[14]

In a banking context, this might be true, but, as Ringo Starr once said, "it don't come easy." There are three forces (or dimensions) that shape the competitive landscape in retail banking:

1) **Customer experience.** I don't like the term "customer experience" because it's so vague, but it's hard to argue against the notion that whatever it is, it's important. However customer experience is defined, though, customer service (or support) is just one component of the overall customer experience. Other components include self-service and the use of the product itself.

2) **Value.** This is a subjective determination (often subconscious, implicit, or qualitative) that consumers make about the extent to which the price they pay for services is worth the benefits reaped.

3) **Product features.** Bankers may think that financial products are commodities (I disagree), but that doesn't mean there aren't distinguishable product features. If the products are commodities, that simply means there is no differentiation in features.

The consumer research I've done has convinced me that there are three groups of banking consumers. Each chooses to do business with a bank that does the best job for them on *one* of the three dimensions (experience, value, or product features), as long as an acceptable level of performance is provided on the other two.

In practice, what this means is that consumers who place the highest emphasis on customer experience are willing to sacrifice—to a certain extent—value and product superiority.

Consumers who consider value to be the most important factor will trade-off (again, to a certain extent) customer experience and product features.

You can figure out for yourself what consumers who put the most emphasis on product features do.

Experience, value, and product are the external dynamics of the retail banking space. There are internal (to the firm, that is) dynamics as well. Competing and conflicting priorities create challenges in allocating resources and creating capabilities. Successful companies demonstrate three attributes:

- **Focus.** Whatever their chosen strategy, successful firms focus their resources on executing that strategy.

- **Alignment.** Successful firms find a way to align business units and functions around a chosen strategy.

- **Discipline.** Successful firms are disciplined in sustaining focus and alignment over a sufficient period of time.

So why is it so hard for banks to pursue a strategy that "creates a competitive advantage through giving outstanding customer care"?

The market isn't big enough. Only so many consumers choose a financial provider for its "outstanding customer care." If you decide to focus on attracting and serving the segment that considers customer experience to be the most important dimension of the three listed above, you might be looking at anywhere from just 10% to 40% of a market as customers/prospects. But we're talking about customer care here, which is only one component of the customer experience—and might not even be an important element of the experience to some portion of this segment.

- **The strategy isn't measurable.** Managers need to be able to gauge two things: 1) To what extent is their chosen strategy a smart strategy, and 2) How well are they executing their chosen strategy. There's no shortage of financial institutions (especially credit unions) who claim to provide superior customer care—with no ability to measure or prove that claim. Without adequate measurement, focus, and alignment discipline becomes impossible to achieve.

- **The strategy isn't specific enough.** A bank that chooses to compete by providing superior customer care still needs to determine the level of quality it needs to provide regarding value and product quality. I'm not saying that this is impossible, but, in practice, focusing on creating an advantage through superior customer care often leads managers to neglect the value and product quality dimensions. The lack of specificity also means that focus, alignment, and discipline is hard to achieve.

- **Organizational structure is a barrier.** This is especially true in banks with more than US$1 billion in assets, whose organizational structure is complicated by departments aligned around products, channels, and geographic regions. Each department has its own budget, and seeks to optimize the return on its spending, with little consideration for the impact of that spending on other departments in the organization.

In the world of retail banking, creating a competitive advantage through giving outstanding customer care isn't likely to happen.

Speed Bumps and Enablers On the Road To the Future

There's a joke in the state of Maine, that if you ask for directions from one of the old codgers that lives there, he'll tell you: "You can't get there from here." It's a comment about the twisting and winding coast line that runs up the coast.

The line might just as well apply to the banking industry. Getting there—to a new business model, new competitive dynamic, and back on the track to success and sustainability—is not a clear path with a well-specified map.

The next section addresses the speed bumps banks face in migrating to a new business model. Speed bumps like: 1) low levels of consumer trust in banks; 2) the lack of consumers' engagement in the management of their financial lives; and 3) resolving the bank branch debate.

Humor Break
Bank Slogans We'd Like to See

I thought it was high time that some banks updated their advertising slogans. Here are my suggestions:

Bank	Old Slogan	New Slogan
Bank of America	Higher Standards	Higher Fees
Capital One	What's in your wallet?	Hand over your wallet.
UBS	You and us.	You BS. So we BS.
Citibank	Live richly	Live richly. We do.
E*Trade	It's your money	It's yOur money

Part II
Speed Bumps On The Road
To The Future

CHAPTER FOUR
DO YOU TRUST ME?

Remember Disney's classic movie, Aladdin? At the beginning of the movie, the princess Jasmine slips out of the palace, and enters the marketplace (a place she's never been to before) and takes a piece of fruit from a vendor's cart. She is chased by the vendor who wants to cut her hand off. Our hero, Aladdin, sees what's going on, and in attempt to pull Jasmine to safety, extends his hand, and says:

"Do you trust me?"

It's at that moment that Jasmine must make a snap decision based on little factual information.

In many respects, this is what many consumers go through when making decisions on who to do business with. They can research and compare products, and, these days, read the reviews and opinions of other people (who may or may not be trustworthy themselves). But at the point of decision, new customers must make a snap decision about whether or not they trust a provider.

For years, by virtue of being a chartered institution, with a branch presence in a community, a bank gained enough trust for consumers to make the decision to do business with it.

That level of trust is gone from the banking industry.

Trust Is The New Black

Craig Newmark, who founded the world's largest online sex bulletin board, once said "trust is the new black."[15] He was referring to news organizations, but his comment is spot on for a range of industries.

There's no shortage of articles commenting on how firm after firm, in industry after industry, has lost the trust of consumers. And no shortage of folks ready to weigh in on what those firms need to do to rebuild that trust.

Wikipedia defines the term black box as, "a device, system or object when it is viewed in terms of its input, output and transfer characteristics *without any knowledge required of its internal workings.*" The italics are mine.

This is what we've got these days when it comes to the concept of trust: The hot topic to opine on (the new black), by people who have no clue about the internal workings of the concept (the black box).

Here's an example. In a MediaPost article titled *Trust is a Beautiful Thing*, Michael Burke, founder and president of appssavvy, states:[16]

> "People trust brands. This is nothing new. What is new is how people are gaining trust in brands and how brands continue to earn that trust. I see two sources of gaining this trust. The first is the source that tells you about the brand. If I hear about something from a friend, the first step in trust is already met."

There are a couple of assertions there that don't hold up to scrutiny.

First, why is hearing about something from a friend a new source of trust? Getting a referral from a friend, family member, or even a stranger isn't something that was invented with the advent of social media.

The second assertion that doesn't hold water is that the "first step in trust is met" with the referral. Why would this be so? It begs the question: If this is the first step, then how many steps are there, and how do we know that?

Burke does go on to say that there is a second source of trust, that brands must earn trust by "recognizing what the consumer expects and not letting them down."

Trust is impacted by many factors, which can be grouped in a number of dimensions (with geeky labels like cognitive factors, institutional factors, symbolic factors, and relationship factors).

The trust factors that social media is going to have the greatest impact on falls into the relationship category. What my research has found, however, is that—according to consumers themselves—relationship factors aren't as important to driving trust as cognitive and institutional factors.

Trust is a complex concept. Reducing it to a black box—or to something with two simple steps to accomplishing—is not helpful to firms looking to rebuild trust with their customers.

Trust-Based Marketing

In a recent issue of the Boston Globe, the front page of one of the sections contained a full-page ad for a bank with the following headline: "Confidence is good. Earning it is better."

The ad highlighted the bank's higher-than-average rate on a 6-month CD, and proclaimed "At XXX Bank, you can feel confident with a short-term CD at a great rate. All from a bank you can trust."

Yes, confidence is good, and earning it is better. But no business, let alone banks, earns confidence by simply offering a good rate. This is true even in normal times.

What makes this ad so insulting is that these are not normal times. Was there nobody at this bank who understood what's going on out there and who could communicate it to the ad agency? Is the ad agency itself that clueless? Did it really believe that simply offering a superior rate is the way to earning [back] the public's confidence?

Glen Urban of MIT was one of the first to write about trust-based marketing and the importance of trust in a customer relationship:[17]

> "Trust-based marketing contrasts with traditional push-based marketing in the assumptions that it makes about a customer. [P]ush-based marketing assumed that customers did not know what was good for them. Under this assumption, firms broadcast their hype to push products onto an ignorant customer base. This contrast between push-based marketing and trust-based marketing parallels McGregor's Theory X and Theory Y. The key is in changing the assumptions that companies hold about their customers."

Trust Is A Two-Way Street

Today, banks apparently embrace the concept of trust-based marketing—it seems like just about every bank exhorts consumers to "trust us." Unfortunately, their actions don't always live up to their words, and many firms fail to recognize that trust is a two-way street. The following is from a recent post from a blogger:

> "I spoke with a bank rep about a $592 fraudulent charge that had been posted to my acct. I filed a dispute against the merchant and was told it would take 5 business days for the matter to be resolved. In the meantime, I was concerned I would incur insufficient fund fees.
>
> The rep informed me I would be able to file a separate dispute once this dispute cleared. Two days later, there was a credit to my acct. for $592. Yeah–problem resolved–or so I thought. I incurred over $300 in insufficient funds fees–Yikes!

As instructed by the rep, I called to file an additional dispute to recover the insufficient funds fees. The rep I filed the original claim with failed to record it on my acct. So they claimed to have no record of a dispute. On top of that, I was informed the (evil) merchant "credited" my account for the unauthorized charge.

Since the merchant "credited" my account, it was no longer considered a fraudulent charge and there was no need for a dispute. What the @%&$?

I got passed off to a manager who informed me the bank wasn't responsible for the insufficient funds fees because there wasn't a record of a dispute. So now you're telling me it's my fault that your people are incompetent?!"

My take: Clearly, a number of things went wrong here. But the most egregious sin is the lack of trust the bank has in its customer. Granted, there is a lot of fraudulent activity happening today. But this bank basically didn't believe its customer when she said she had called to file the claim. In effect, it called her a liar.

Here we have a bank that tells customers and prospects in its ads and marketing messages to "trust us." And what does it do? Turns around and mistrusts its own customers.

A simple review of this blogger's account would likely have provided clues as to whether or not she was trying to commit some fraud. But it should never have even come to that. The bank—without batting an eyelash—should have apologized and told her it was sorry and that it would credit her account for the fees. And then look into the legitimacy of the situation. We're talking $300 here.

What's sad about this situation is that if this customer is a professional or small business owner, she's likely to get cross-sell offers from the bank to open investment accounts or a small business account. What are the chances that she'll respond to these offers? Slim to none. Apparently, many banks don't understand that:

1) Banks have to identify and act on the moments of truth that occur. This was a moment of truth. The bank didn't identify it, and (in this case) couldn't rectify it. The result was maybe not a lost customer, but probably a customer who's unlikely to grow her relationship.

2) To get trust, you have to give trust.

Interpreting the Trust Surveys

There is no shortage of studies demonstrating the low level of trust that Americans have in banks. For the past decade, Gallup has measured "net sentiment" by capturing the percentage of consumers that give the industry a positive, neutral, and negative rating, and subtracting the negative percentage from the positive percentage.

From 2001 through 2007, banks' net sentiment score was positive, reaching a high of 39% in 2006. Since 2008, however, net sentiment has been negative, hitting a low of -28% in 2010 and 2012. It rebounded in 2013, but was still negative, with 33% of consumers rating banks positively, but 43% rating them negatively (Figure 4.1).

Figure 4.1

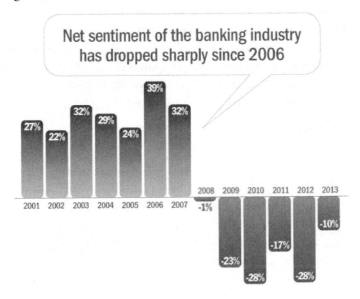

Source: Gallup, The Financial Brand

How did consumers come to these views—and a low level of trust—regarding banks? Perhaps you think that people's trust opinions are shaped by word-of-mouth (not that anyone would ever embellish a story to make it sound better or worse, would they?).

Research that I've done suggests otherwise. What consumers think about their primary bank influences their perception about the industry as a whole. The more highly consumers rate their primary bank on an attribute, the more likely they are to ascribe that attribute to banks in general.[18] And vice versa.

Among consumers who think that their primary bank is "not at all easy to do business with," two-thirds think banks, in general, are not at all easy to do business with. More than half (55%) who said their primary bank was somewhat easy to do business with also said banks in general were somewhat easy to do business with. Of those who had no opinion on whether or not their primary bank is easy to do business with, about eight in ten have no opinion about banks in general. And of consumers who said their primary bank was extremely easy to do business with, about eight in ten said banks in general were either somewhat or extremely easy to do business with (Figure 4.2).

Figure 4.2

		To what extent is **your primary bank easy to do business with?**				
		Not at all	Very little	No opinion	Somewhat	Extremely
To what extent are **banks in general easy to do business with?**	Not at all	**65%**	19%	2%	3%	5%
	Very little	20%	**61%**	6%	13%	7%
	No opinion	15%	14%	**79%**	21%	9%
	Somewhat			11%	**55%**	47%
	Extremely		7%	2%	8%	**32%**

Source: *The Financial Brand, Aite Group*

There is a similar pattern regarding "friendly and helpful service reps" and "the extent to which banks clearly describe their services" (Figure 4.3 and Figure 4.4).

Figure 4.3

		To what extent is **your primary bank friendly and helpful?**				
		Not at all	Very little	No opinion	Somewhat	Extremely
To what extent are **banks in general friendly and helpful?**	Not at all	**100%**	5%	1%	1%	4%
	Very little	20%	**52%**	1%	7%	4%
	No opinion	5%	34%	**84%**	17%	6%
	Somewhat		9%	11%	**65%**	45%
	Extremely			4%	9%	**40%**

Source: *The Financial Brand, Aite Group*

Figure 4.4

		To what extent does **your primary bank clearly explain its services?**				
		Not at all	Very little	No opinion	Somewhat	Extremely
To what extent do **banks in general explain their services?**	Not at all	82%	14%	1%		7%
	Very little	6%	52%	7%	13%	9%
	No opinion		18%	74%	13%	11%
	Somewhat	11%	16%	17%	68%	38%
	Extremely			2%	6%	35%

Source: The Financial Brand, Aite Group

What Is Trust?

Merriam-Webster defines trust as "assured reliance on the character, ability, strength, or truth of someone or something." As this definition implies, trust is a multi-dimensional concept. Based on its research on the drivers of trust and its impact on personal and business relationships, Plenitudes defines trust as having four dimensions:

- **Symbolic.** This dimension appeals to emotions and feelings like reputation, image, and consideration, which contribute to a sense of trust. "I can trust the institution because it has the same values as I do."

- **Relationship.** This dimension encompasses the facets of empathy, intimacy and sincerity that contribute to trust. "To trust an institution, it needs to understand me and my situation."

- **Institutional.** The organizational structure and rules that shape the behaviors of an institution and its representatives. "I can trust the institution because its rules make it credible."

- **Cognitive.** The capabilities and experiences that a person or institution must have in order to be trusted.

"I can trust the institution because I know it can do what it promises to do."

Consumers assign greater importance to rational factors (like cognitive and institutional dimensions) than to emotional factors (e.g., symbolic and relationship dimensions). As a result, in order to build trust, consumers require the following:

- **Competency and clarity.** Overall, the cognitive dimension was rated as the most important among respondents. Forty-five percent of consumers surveyed said that competency is extremely important in building trust, while 43% said that clear policies—i.e., those that are easily understandable—are extremely important driver of trust.

- **Responsibility and transparency.** Among the institutional attributes, nearly half of respondents cited responsibility, and 41% mentioned transparency (i.e., clear policies that don't deceive or trick them) as extremely important.

- **Honesty and sincerity.** Fifty-three percent of consumers deemed honesty—a relationship attribute—an extremely important driver of trust, while sincerity was on the extremely important list of 40% of the respondents.

Not surprisingly, consumers rated the cognitive and institutional dimensions as more important than the symbolic and relationship. Consumers typically overstate the influence of rational factors on their decisions, and downplay the non-rational (or emotional).

Banks' efforts to build (or rebuild) trust often focus on the symbolic and relationship dimensions. Branding efforts, for example, often stress banks' altruism (e.g., Bank of America's television commercials about its community contributions) or the bank's friendliness, empathy, and sincerity (e.g., Citizen's Bank ad where an employee helps a customer take her grocery packages to her car), which are relationship attributes. Because advertising does little to impact the perceptions that consumers have of these banks' cognitive and institutional abilities, the ads will only have a limited impact on consumers' trust in the banks.

Aite Group's research also identified the drivers of mistrust. Unlike the drivers of trust, where two dimensions emerged as more important than the other two, the four dimensions were more on a par regarding their impact on consumer mistrust. What can lead to mistrust of providers and institutions?

- **Insufficient skill, knowledge, and experience.** Survey respondents identified this as the most important cognitive attribute. In addition, more than a third (36%) of respondents said that mistrust is created when firms don't provide the products and services they promise to.

- **Low moral or ethical standards.** Nearly four in 10 consumers believe this institutional attribute is extremely important in causing mistrust.

- **Experiencing problems.** Nearly half of respondents believe that experiencing a problem with a provider or institution is an extremely important driver of mistrust. Doing things that aren't in the best interest of customers was cited as an extremely important driver by 39% of consumers.

- **Dissatisfaction.** Simply feeling dissatisfied is a strong driver of mistrust. Among symbolic attributes, dissatisfaction was closely followed by the perception that one is being forced to make decisions that he or she doesn't want to make.

Bottom line: You can't advertise your way to trust.

Are Financial Ads Trustworthy?

Maybe it doesn't even matter that you can't advertise your way to trust. People don't believe financial services ads. At least that's the conclusion of one study.

Among five major industries, Americans trust soft drink advertising the most, according to a Harris Poll.[19] Thirty-four percent of adults said that they trust soft drink advertising, 22% trust fast food ads, 18% trust pharma ads, 14% trust car ads, and 13% trust financial services ads (Table 4.1).

Table 4.1

Percentage of consumers that consider ads from the following types of companies to be the "most trustworthy"

	Total	18–34 years old	35–44 years old	45–54 years old	55+ years old
Soft drink	34%	39%	40%	32%	27%
Fast food	22%	17%	22%	27%	24%
Pharmaceutical	18%	20%	14%	15%	19%
Automobile	14%	12%	13%	14%	16%
Financial services	13%	13%	10%	12%	14%

Source: Harris Research

Respondents were asked "of the five categories, which do you trust the most?" (Add up the five numbers in each column). Do you see the problem here?

Assume for a moment that there were 100 kids in your high school graduating class. Your GPA was 99.6 (out of 100). Pretty good, eh? I'd say so. But further assume that GPA only put you in fifth place (the four nerds who did better than you had 99.7, 99.8, 99.9, and 100 averages, respectively).

Were you the worst performer? Out of the top 5, yes. Does that mean you did poorly? No.

This is the problem with the Harris study. Financial services ads were not deemed untrustworthy. They were simply ranked the least trustworthy out of the five categories that the researcher asked about.

Which raises a whole host of questions: Why did they choose those categories? Why didn't they ask about other categories? Why didn't they simply ask how trustworthy each category's ads are?

Does this mean that bank ads are trustworthy? No. But we can't conclude from the data that they're not trustworthy. It's wrong to simply assume that because there's a lack of trust in banks, that people find the ads not trustworthy.

Despite the flawed research, I'm not sure what people were thinking when they responded to the study. Do you mean to tell me that ads from Taco Bell, which attempt to position its fast food as a "healthy choice," are trustworthy? Or that pharma ads like the ones from Enzyte that promise body part growth are trustworthy?

Ads from financial services aren't any less trustworthy than any other industry's ads. [Cut to Don Henley's Dirty Laundry: "Kick 'em when they're up, kick 'em when they're down....."]

The Customer Relationship Infrastructure

I would guess that you're sitting inside a nice comfortable building right now (if you're out by a pool, drinking a pina colada, then: 1) I hate you, and 2) Why are you reading this out by the pool?).

Are you worried that the building that you're sitting in is going to fall down and crumble around you?

Of course not. You're confident that there is a foundation upon which the building was built that will keep it from falling down, and that there's an infrastructure that enables you to do things like hang pictures on the wall, or draw power from outlets in the wall.

The concept of an "infrastructure" is very common in business, especially in the world of IT. The IT department in your company understands that your firm needs an IT infra-structure—servers, routers, PCs printers, etc.—upon which applications run.

The IT department also knows—after many years of trying—that you can't calculate an ROI on the investment in IT infrastructure. The return comes from the applications that use the infrastructure—not the infrastructure itself.

All of this is gobbledygook to marketers. While marketers might understand that there needs to be an infrastructure to support the CRM apps they use, the concept of an infrastructure to support customer relationships is a foreign concept to them.

While marketers are obsessed with figuring out what to do with social media, or how to tack the label "social" onto their CRM investments, there is something that they are missing: Building strong customer relationships require a "infrastructure" upon which to build those relationships.

Conceptually, a customer relationship infrastructure boils down to two things: Engagement and trust.

It's no different in a business context than it is in a personal context. Strong personal relationships are built when two people engage (in meaningful ways) and develop a bond of trust.

The word "meaningful" is critical in that previous sentence. You might "engage" everyday with the person behind the counter at Dunkin Donuts where you buy your coffee every morning, but there really isn't much of a relationship there because those interactions aren't very meaningful.

What this means, from a practical perspective, will be very troublesome for marketers.

If marketers need to build a customer relationship infra-structure, that means that they will need to make investments in things that—by definition—will not produce a return on that investment.

I think this is going to be the case with many social media investments. The benefit (just because an investment doesn't produce a return does not mean that it doesn't produce benefits) of these efforts will be to engage customers and prospects more often, and in more meaningful ways, than firms have been able to do in the past.

And the result of that meaningful engagement will be higher levels of trust, which will ultimately result in stronger levels of relationship, as measured by loyalty and purchase behavior. But attributing the increase in loyalty or purchase behavior directly to the investments in social media will be a tricky proposition, since direct marketing and sales efforts will still continue to be executed.

A good example of this kind of investment in the world of banking is PFM. Many banks will be searching for the "ROI on PFM" this year, and many banks will be either be frustrated by what they find or will fall prey to what I like to call the "correlation delusion" (i.e., they will attribute an increase in retention among PFM users to PFM even though many other factors may have played a role).

If, instead, banks look at PFM as an engagement platform— a way to interact meaningfully (i.e., helping users make smart decisions about their financial lives, and not just pushing offers at them)—then PFM becomes an integral component of the customer relationship infrastructure.

This is a big change in perception for marketers. IT had to go through it. Marketing will too.

This also means that measuring engagement and trust will become important, as well. Since investments in the infrastructure won't produce a direct return, the benefits will have to be measured in terms of improvements in engagement and trust.

And guess what? Measuring how many pages web site visitors hit, or the amount of time they spend on the site won't cut it as a measure of engagement. Nor will the "time spent interacting with an ad," which seems to be the advertising community's favorite measure of engagement.

Trust measurement will evolve as well. Banks can't simply ask "do you trust us?"

Rebuilding Trust With A Customer Relationship Infrastructure

While there are a lot of things that banks could do to rebuild trust, any action or initiative must demonstrate:

- **Transparency.** If the CEO of a company goes on TV and tells the world the future of the firm looks bright, and then two days later other banks are picking at it like vultures on roadkill, then that firm is not transparent. Consumers (not to mention investors) are sick and tired of this stuff. Come clean about your financial situation. And come clean about your product quality. And your fees. Be transparent. Consumers know the difference.

- **Tangibility.** Recently, a bank ran a series of ads showing someone wrestling—literally—with some aspect of their financial life: a wallet, purse, or checkbook. The only text on the page—the headline—says "take control of your finances."[20] What does that mean? Exactly what is this bank proposing to DO to actually help us "take control"? Aspirational messages are nice, but banks need to be more tangible about delivering on this stuff.

- **Competency.** Someday, I will get a call from my account manager at my bank, asking me to talk with an adviser from the investment firm that they recently acquired. My response will be "You want me to talk to an adviser from a firm that did such a lousy job managing its own money that it nearly went out of business before you guys scooped them up for 10% of the value they were worth a year earlier?" A bank branch rep I spoke to recently couldn't even answer basic questions about the changes in FDIC coverage. My point: To improve their reputations, banks must re-prove their basic competency regarding financial matters.

Banks should:

1) **Improve their sales process.** Over the past few years, many bank executives have discussed creating a sales culture in their organizations. What a waste of time. It's not the culture that needs to be changed—it's the skill sets within banks.

   Cognitive attributes were rated as the most important drivers of trust, yet respondents believe that these attributes are the least likely ones to describe their banks extremely well. These attributes relate closely to what occurs during sales interactions: Clearly explaining products and services, making rates and fees crystal clear, acknowledging the quality of competitors' products and services, and letting prospects and customers know when it's a bad time to buy the bank's products.

   Improving the bank's abilities to deliver on these cognitive attributes has multiple benefits. It improves: 1) the success of the sales interactions; 2) customers' trust in the bank; and 3) customers' trust in the bank early in the customer's tenure with the bank, increasing the likelihood that the customer will want to do more business with the bank.

2) **Redesign the onboarding process.** The American Bankers Association urged banks to "create a structured [on-boarding] program to cross-sell new people and lock them in—so that deposits don't go out the back door as fast as they come in the front."[21] This is based on faulty logic. First, it presumes that customers can be "locked-in." The reality is that switching banks—or at the least moving money between banks—has never been easier. Second, it ignores the realities of what it takes to grow a customer relationship—namely, a high degree of trust in the bank on the part of the customer.

Banks should downplay cross-selling in their on-boarding programs, and focus more on helping new customers make the best use of the products or services they just opened. This requires a more sophisticated approach to messaging and customer contact cadence than the welcome kit that comprises the onboarding process for many banks today.

3)   **Track referral behavior—not intention.** Banks need not survey customers to determine the extent to which they trust the bank. The last thing a bank wants to do now is add another metric to track on top of customer satisfaction and net promoter score. But banks do need to focus more on tracking the referrals made by their customers, and focus less on customers' intention to refer.

Referral behavior is an indicator that a customer has a high degree of trust in the bank, and not just a basic level. An increase in referrals is a signal that trust levels in the bank are increasing, as well. And it's an opportunity for the bank to thank the referrer and re-strengthen that relationship as well.

4)   **Collaborate to rebuild trust in the banking industry.** Recently, Coca-Cola ran a marketing campaign in which it gave away a free bottle of its new Vault soda to consumers who purchased a bottle of Mountain Dew (a competitor's product). The campaign likely drove up sales of Mountain Dew. Was it a smart move?

Yes, because it drove up category sales. By incentivizing consumers to drink citrus-type soda, Coca-Cola spurred interest in this category of soft drink. When demand for the category is strong, they'll slug it out with Mountain Dew for category supremacy.

This is analogous to what banks need to do right now: Work together to build and rebuild consumer trust in banks and in the financial services industry. *Then* slug it out.

HUMOR BREAK
SONGS FOR THE CITI

According to the Wall Street Journal:

> "The banking industry has spent countless hours and dollars trying to make up for the damage done by the financial crisis. Banks have run feel-good ads, waged aggressive lobbying campaigns, even sponsored bike-rental programs. Now Citigroup is trying a new tactic: singing. On national TV. Citigroup's London office opened its skyscraper to a BBC crew filming the popular TV series 'The Choir.'"

Apparently, the group's repertoire includes something from a Delibes opera, something from someone named Mary Mary, and a Michael Jackson tune.

Boring! Here's what the bankers should be singing:

10. Animals, "We Gotta Get Out Of This Place"

9. Bee Gees, "Stayin' Alive"

8. Bob Dylan, "The Times They Are a-Changin'"

7. Jane's Addiction, "Been Caught Stealin'"

6. Led Zeppelin, "Dazed and Confused"

5. Barry McGuire, "Eve of Destruction"

4. The Surfaris, "Wipe Out"

3. The Smiths, "Heaven Knows I'm Miserable Now"

2. The Temptations, "Ain't Too Proud to Beg"

And the number one song Citi should sing:

1. Stevie Wonder, "Living for the Citi".

Chapter Five
Overcoming The Customer
Engagement Hurdle

An article in an advertising industry publication quoted the CMO of a large bank as saying, "we want to become an iconic brand that people love."[22] And I want to be the starting quarterback of the New England Patriots and have beautiful models throw themselves at me.

And you know what? I may have a better chance of achieving my fantasy than the bank CMO does of achieving his/hers.

The CMO went on to say "through ongoing brand tracking, we know we always outperform our peers when it comes to being emotionally relevant to people. The new campaign gives us a unique opportunity to talk about who we are."

Note to CMO: Nobody cares who you are. To become an iconic brand that people love, it takes a lot more than a new ad campaign.

You cannot advertise your way to greatness.

Sure, some iconic brands—Apple and Nike, for instance— have memorable advertising campaigns that build on, support, or enhance their iconicosity (I made up that word).

But when you look at those firms, there's something else that helps them achieve high iconicosity. In Apple's case its customers who are really into technology, and in Nike's case it's athletes and aspiring athletes.

What does a bank have? Checking account fanatics? Bill pay aficionados?

What Apple and Nike have—that banks don't—are engaged customers. Customers that are engaged, not just with those firms, but with the products and services they sell.

Americans are just not that engaged in financial services.

What is Customer Engagement?

The Advertising Research Foundation (ARF) defines engagement as:[23]

"Turning on a prospect to a brand idea enhanced by the surrounding context."

Here's a picture of the guy who came up with that definition:

Just kidding. But I do wonder what they were smoking when they came up with that definition. "Turning on" prospects? "Enhanced by the surrounding context"? What does that mean?

Robert Passikoff, President of Brand Keys, predicted that engagement would "continue to insert itself between traditional marketing activities and an increasing demand for return-on-investment assessments, and occupy a good deal of marketers' and advertisers' attentions."[24]

That may very well be, but a poor definition of the term will keep the concept limited to being just a buzzword. The term is narrowly defined by the marketing community as relating to just interactions that occur on online and mobile channels, and, for some marketers, just interactions with ads. I prefer to think of customer engagement as:

> "Repeated—and satisfying—interactions that strengthen the emotional connection a consumer has with a brand, product, or company."

When marketers think of "customer engagement," they should be thinking about how engaged the customer is with the company, product, or brand. The level of involvement with the website—or with a particular ad (online or offline)—is just one dimension of a customer's engagement.

Customer engagement encompasses a number of dimensions:

- **Product involvement.** A customer who doesn't care about the product, is likely to be less committed or emotionally attached to the firm providing the product.

- **Frequency of purchase.** A customer who purchases more frequently may be more engaged than other customers.

- **Frequency of service interactions.** Branding experts like to say that repeated, positive interactions lead to brand affinity. And they're right to a certain extent, but....

- **Types of interactions. ...not all types of interactions are created equally.** Checking account balances is a very different type of interaction than a request to help choose between product or service options.

- **Channel behavior.** Customers who interact in multiple channels may be demonstrating a greater level of engagement (or they may just be looking for the most expedient way to be finished and done with the company).

- **Referral behavior/intention.** Customers who actually refer a firm to friends and family are more engaged than those who simply intend to provide a referral.

- **Velocity.** The rate of change in the indicators listed above may be a signal of engagement.

The result is a metric that is immediately useful in helping marketers address some strategic questions about their marketing and customer strategy, when segmenting customers by their level of customer engagement and breadth of relationship with the company or brand (Figure 5.1).

Figure 5.1

Degree of customer engagement

		Low	High
Breadth of relationship	High	Who are these attrition risks and what can be done to retain them?	How do these customers differ from the others?
	Low	Why aren't these customers engaged, what can be done to engage them?	What needs aren't being met for these highly engaged customers?

Source: Author

Broadly measuring engagement (beyond the advertising purview) helps marketers address:

- **Which customers aren't engaged?** Marketers may uncover demographic trends when evaluating engagement. For example, a bank may find that it is engaging younger consumers more effectively than older consumers (who may represent a more affluent set of prospects).

- **Which customers are most engaged?** Marketers can improve campaign response rates by targeting engaged customers who are more likely than other customers to do more business with the bank.

- **Which customers are less engaged?** These customers may represent attrition risks, requiring preventive measures to retain them.

- **Which customers migrated between quadrants?** Movements between quadrants can signal problems or opportunities.

- **What is the profit impact of engaging customers?** By analyzing the profitability of customers in each of the quadrants, marketers can model the potential profit impact of running marketing programs that increase engagement.

Why Engagement Matters

Without engagement, there is no relationship. This is true whether we're talking about a business to consumer relationship, or a relationship between two people.

There are two aspects to engagement: Quantity and quality. How often you engage, and how meaningful those engagements are. Duration of contact, however, means nothing.

Ever notice how people who serve in the military—in battle—develop close relationships in a short period of time, and how those relationships often persist after their tour of duty is over? That's because, even though the duration of their engagement is short, the quality of the engagement—the highly emotional situations they're involved in—is high.

Conversely, imagine that every morning before you go to work, you stop off at a coffee shop to get a cup of coffee. Over time, the folks at the coffee shop begin to know who you are, and as soon as they see you getting out of your car, they've already started to make your favorite latte, and it's ready and waiting as soon as you get in. Just how you like it. Short duration, not a particularly high emotional content, but repeated, satisfying interactions build engagement.

Marketers are, for the most part, clueless to this. Many wrongly obsess over how long people spend looking at their ad, or how long they spend on the marketer's website.

To understand why quality of engagement is more important than duration, and even quantity, listen to John Gottman, the Executive Director of the Relationship Institute:

"Good relationships aren't about clear communication—they're about small moments of attachment and intimacy."

This is true whether we're talking about personal relationships or business-to-customer relationships. Yet many marketers focus more on their "story," and getting it across to customers and prospects.

That's too bad, because a marketer's story isn't worth diddly-squat. The only "story" that matters is the customer's story, and that story doesn't come from advertising, it comes from being engaged with a firm, brand, or product.

Trying to impose or enforce definitions of commonly used buzzwords is a tricky sport, and I'm loathe to do it, but here it is. Engagement isn't how long someone spends on your site, or looking at your ad, it isn't channel-specific, and it can't be boiled down to a single, behavioral measure. It's a series of interactions that strengthen a customer's emotional connection to a brand, product or company.

Customer Engagement in Banking

An American Banker editorial on customer engagement in banking opined:[25]

"I can't help thinking the money management moment has passed and that, moving forward, engagement banking—a future model for the industry that PFM is a big part of—would benefit from less engagement. This might reflect my lifelong aversion to charts and graphs. Or it could be related to a suspicion that many financial firms want to 'engage' with me simply to obtain information marketable to a third party. This could be one more instance where terminology is failing the industry, given that the word 'engagement' denotes a level of commitment not all consumers may be looking for in their banking relationships."

My take: The sentiments expressed in the editorial are understandable. American Banker even cites a study that found that nearly half of consumers surveyed want technology to simplify their lives. But the opinions expressed in the editorial reflect a different definition of engagement from what I propose (i.e., "repeated and satisfying interactions that strengthen the emotional connection a consumer has with a brand, product, or company").

The key phrase is "emotional connection." Simply interacting more often with a customer is not engagement. Only meaningful interactions create, or build on, the emotional connection.

Making offers within the online banking platform or on a mobile device—regardless of how relevant the offers are, they are just not meaningful interactions for many consumers. The author of the editorial talks about her "lifelong aversion to charts and graphs." She's not alone. Lots of people couldn't care less about charting their current or future spending. Expense categorization? A chore.

So yes, people want technology to "simplify" their lives. What they're really saying is "I want technology to do the things I don't want to do" and "I want technology to alleviate and fix the problems I have with the companies I do business with."

Aite Group segmented consumers into three groups based on the frequency with which they performed 13 financial activities. One in five consumers were categorized as Highly Active (or engaged in the management of their financial life), 50% were Moderately Active, and 30% were Inactive (i.e., not at all engaged).[26]

The differences in financial behaviors between the segments are stark. Three-quarters or more of the Highly Active consumers forecast and categorize their spending, as well as maintain a household budget. Less than half the Moderately Active perform these activities on a regular basis, and among the Inactive, not even one in 10 do them on a monthly basis.

The 30% of consumers who fall into the Inactive segment are simply not managing their financial lives.

Bottom line: The things that banks are doing to generate "engagement" among their customers—PFM tools, merchant-funded offers, Facebook pages, blog posts, tweets, and YouTube videos—are unwanted by about 80% of the population.

The solution isn't less engagement. It's more engagement—more meaningful engagement. Interactions that not only strengthen the emotional connection that the customer has with the bank, but that deepen their involvement in the management of their financial life.

Lack of consumer engagement in the management of their financial lives has a downside for banks. Among consumers who aren't highly engaged in the management of their financial lives, the overwhelming majority don't want their primary bank or credit union to help them manage their finances.[27]

The Impact of Customer Engagement in Banking

The level of customer engagement impacts banks' bottom lines. Compared to other consumers, the consumers in the Highly Engaged segment are more likely to:

- **Grow their relationship with their primary financial institution.** According to the Aite Group survey, just 4% of Inactive consumers expanded their relationship (by increasing balances and/or number of accounts) with their primary financial institution in the 12 months preceding the survey. Among Moderately Active consumers, that percentage was 11%, and among Highly Active consumers it was 14%.

- **Refer their FI.** Highly Active consumers are 1.5 times more likely to refer their primary financial institution to family/friends than Moderately Active consumers, and twice as likely as Inactive consumers.

- **Use and reap the benefits of PFM.** Nearly two-thirds of Highly Active consumers use an online PFM tool, in contrast to just one in four Moderately Active consumers, and one in 10 Inactive consumers. More importantly, Highly Active consumers reap the benefits of PFM. Among PFM users, Highly Active consumers are four times as likely as other consumers to have saved on fees or interest payments as the result of using PFM.

Chapter Six
Pruning The Branches

Recent trends don't portend a healthy future for bank branches, do they? From about the beginning of time, through to about 1992, everyone—and I mean everyone—who did business with a bank, went into a bank branch at least once a month (Figure 6.1).

Figure 6.1

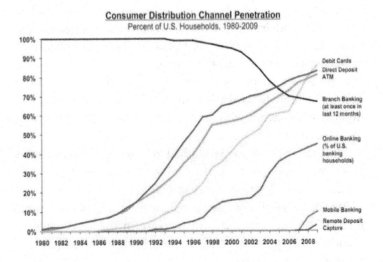

Source: FDIC

In the ensuring 16 years, that percentage fell to less than 70%. "Branches are dead!" proclaimed the Branch Abolitionists, also pointing to the number of bank branches that have closed over the past 10 years.

My take: Pointing to bank branch closures as a signal of the death of branches is like saying that someone who has lost weight is dying.

Actually, that might be a terrible analogy. A closer inspection of what's going on with bank branches is that banks aren't really slimming down—they're bulking up.

Among the top 10 banks, between 2009 and 2012, the number of bank branches declined by 1%. The biggest losers (not a pejorative statement) were Bank of America and Regions Bank who shed 10% and 9% of their branches, respectively. BB&T and PNC were the big gainers, growing branch count 23% and 10%.

But the real story in bank branches isn't the number of branches. It's the change in the distribution of branch size.

Among the 10 largest banks in the United States, the number of branches with less than US$10m in deposits dropped by 15%. In contrast, the number of branches with more than US$100m in deposits grew 7%, and the number of bank branches with US$50-100m in deposits increased by 4%. In addition to the decline in branches with less than US$10m in deposits, the number of branches with US$10-30m in deposits receded by 4% respectively.

In 2012, the top 10 banks had 663 more branches with US$100m+ in deposits than they did in 2009. And they had 930 fewer branches with less than US$10m.

This branch bulking was consistent across the top 10 banks. Eight of the 10 banks saw an increase in the percentage of branches with greater than US$100m in deposits, despite the variation across banks.

For example, even though Bank of America's branch count declined by 10% between 2009 and 2012, the decline in branches with more than US$100m in deposits totaled just 8 branches. As a result, the percentage of their branches with more than $100m in deposits increased from 54% to 59%.

At US Bank, which had just 17% of branches with $100m+ in 2009, that percentage grew to 25% in 2012. Wells Fargo also increased its distribution of branches to the US$100m+ category to 54% in 2012, up from 48% in 2009.

The decline in the less than US$10m category is striking. SunTrust closed nearly 40% of its branches in this segment, Wells Fargo closed more than a third, and Bank of America and RBS closed one in four.

While I'm not a big fan of banks investing big dollars in branches, the proclamations of the death of bank branches—that rely on total bank branch numbers—are misguided.

Branches aren't dying. Small branches are dying. Banks are bulking up the remaining branches.

Do Branches Matter?

In a recent Economic Commentary titled *Do Bank Branches Matter Anymore?*, the Federal Reserve Bank of Cleveland wrote that bank branches matter because a local presence in a market—i.e., bank branches—enables a bank to gather better data about local conditions and make better lending decisions.[28] The authors wrote:

> "Bank-customer relationships can overcome adverse selection in lending decisions. For banks, interactions with customers allow them to gather information on a customer, so-called soft information, which is not easily captured in a credit score. Banks operating in a local market are also more likely to have information on the local economy, giving them a context from which they can evaluate the future prospects of a borrower that is not readily available to an out-of-market lender."

Because gathering "soft" information is difficult to do without a physical presence in a local market, the closing of a bank branch is different from the closing of a grocery store. One can still buy oranges, perhaps at a higher cost, by traveling farther to a different grocery store. But one cannot always get a loan by traveling to a distant lender.

We find that low-income homebuyers who obtain their mortgages from banks with branches in their neighborhoods are less likely to default than homebuyers who use banks without a branch in the area or mortgage brokers. These findings suggest that a physical presence gives banks the opportunity to get to know distressed areas better and channel resources to people who can manage them best."

My take: The Fed is wrong about:

1. **Knowing a market.** "Knowing" a market doesn't come from having physical offices (or branches) in a market. "Knowing" a market comes from developing a systemic business capability that captures data about a market, and on the impact and results of business decisions made in that market over a period of time.

   The "soft" information that the authors refer to—information about spending habits of individual borrowers—is no more accessible to a bank with a physical presence in a market than to a bank without a physical presence.

   In fact, I would argue that an Internet-only bank whose customers are heavy users of debit cards actually have better "soft" data regarding their customers financial lives than a branch-oriented bank who customers still rely heavily on cash and checks. Why? Banks' ability to categorize debit card transactions is more advanced than their ability to analyze check transactions.

2. **Correlation and causation.** The Fed is confusing correlation with causation. It might be true that "low-income homebuyers who obtain mortgages from banks with

branches in their neighborhoods are less likely to default than homebuyers who use banks without a branch in the area or mortgage brokers."

But the only way that the absence of bank branches would be the cause of the default is if applicants applied to both bricks-and-mortar and Internet-only banks, and were turned down by the bricks-and-mortar banks and accepted by the branch-less ones. This doesn't seem very likely.

It's hard to tell from the article, but it appears that the authors looked at data from a selected number of counties in Ohio, comparing 2002 to 2010. Had they looked at California, Florida, or Texas, they would have found very different results. In addition, as the authors note, bank branches "have been disappearing in some major metropolitan areas."

With the economic conditions that existed between 2008 and 2010, it's hard to conclude that the increase in loan defaults is caused by branch disappearances.

If the purpose of the article is to convince banks that in order to improve their lending business they need to expand their branch presence, I have to disagree.

Looking ahead, the opportunity for banks to gather "soft" information about customers and markets will not come from a branch presence. Instead, it will come from the growth in the use of mobile technology—specifically for mobile banking and mobile payments will give the banks much greater insight into spending habits and trends in the markets they do business in.

Why Bank Branches Suck

Chris Skinner, author of *The Digital Bank*, argues that:[29]

"Branches are banks' retail stores but were designed for money. They were designed to handle physical forms of cash and cheques, as secure transaction centres. This is the core challenge of why everyone thinks branches will disappear. Because they are not retail stores engaging the brand community but transaction centres run like some administration process."

In imagining—in his words—"how the branch experience becomes a retail experience fit for 2013 and beyond," Skinner identifies a few examples:

- Washington Mutual (Occasio) and Umpqua removed teller counters and opened the dialogue over a face-to-face table form.

- Caja Navarro and ING Direct instigated "community engagement" (Chris' words) by having open house sessions. Caja Navarro offered evening classes in their stores including hair styling and flower arranging, and ING Direct offered sessions where anyone could just ask questions like: "How does a mortgage work?"

- Umpqua allows branches to be booked in the evening for cocktail parties or business meetings.

My take: These are all interesting examples of alternative (and creative) uses of branch space, but do little or nothing to prove that branches are an economically viable (i.e., profitable) way of doing business for banks.

Skinner cites a Bloomberg article that appeared shortly after Apple launched its retail stores:

"Jobs thinks he can do a better job than experienced retailers. Problem is, the numbers don't add up. I give them two years before they're turning out the lights on a very painful and expensive mistake."

Bet that guy wishes he could take those words back. But the important point is why he was wrong. So-called "experienced retailers" were experienced at selling consumer products (clothing, jewelry, shoes)—not technology products.

At the time of Apple's launching of retail stores, there were two frames of reference: 1) How existing retailers sold consumer products, and 2) How existing technology companies sold technology products. Apple stores didn't fit either frame of reference, and hence, geniuses like the one at Bloomberg wrote them off.

Apple reinvented the way technology products were sold. (It took a couple of tweaks, they didn't get it right on the first try). What Apple has got right, regarding the sale of technology products, is creating a retail experience that is:

- **Visual.** People want to see the product.

- **Tactile.** People want to touch and use the product.

- **Informative.** People want to talk to store reps who know about the products.

- **Advocative** (I made that word up). People want reps who will recommend products that are right for the customer, not just for the store.

- **Lean.** The buying process is fast, with a minimal number of steps. No waiting in cash register lines. Fast and lean.

Apple stores are successful because—for the most part—they succeed at accomplishing these five things. And it doesn't hurt that the products Apple sells are products that consumers consider to be very important in their personal lives.

This is why bank branches suck: They don't accomplish these five objectives (yeah, I know, if I flip-flopped #2 and #3 we could say that branches aren't VITAL. I hate stupid acronyms). Granted, banks are handicapped here.

It's tough to "see" and "touch" most financial products and services. You used to be able to touch a checking account—i.e., your checkbook—but nobody does that anymore, and you didn't get that until days after opening your account anyway.

And, for the vast majority of consumers (at least here in the US), although money is really really important to us, our choice of financial products and providers isn't. We spend more time figuring out what restaurant to eat out at on a Saturday night than we do which bank we do business with.

There is, however, no excuse for why banks don't meet the informative and advocative hurdles.

This is also why the various "branch of the future" concepts fall short: They don't do anything to reinvent the way financial products are sold.

The branchlet concept is great—as are the hair styling, flower arranging, yoga classes, and cocktail party ideas. But they only address the efficiency (cost) side of the coin, not the effectiveness (sales) side.

Skinner was spot on in describing the branch as a "transaction centre run like some administration process." Hair styling and flower arranging classes, however, is just lipstick on a pig.

Skinner was also spot on in suggesting that banks should "combine the two worlds: the retail store and the remote experience." But I've yet to see a "branch of the future" concept that does that. Most branch-of-the-future concepts bring more technology into the branch, but few (if any) do anything to integrate the branch experience with the remote experience.

Banks have two huge hurdles to overcome in order to make branches profitable:

1. **Redefining how financial products are sold.** Sitting down at a desk with someone who may or may not be well informed about the products, asking me personal questions about my finances that I have no interest in sharing, talking about how they may or may not be right for me... it's a crappy experience.

2. **Getting more people engaged in the management of their financial lives.** Skinner talks about "using stores as

a method of building a sense of community around your brand." It works for Apple because people really care a lot about their choice of smartphones, PCs, and music devices. You don't get brand engagement without product category engagement.

There's a chicken-and-egg situation with this last point. If I'm not engaged in managing my financial life, why would I go into a branch to learn how a mortgage works? (Unless, of course, there was a free meal there. Free drinks, even better. Offer Macallan 18 year old Scotch and I'll even come in for the hair styling and basket weaving classes).

Apple may have reinvented the way technology products are sold, but the company is successful with its retail strategy because they get people in the door. Ironically, when new products are released, there's often a line, and people can't get in. But you know what I mean.

Flower arranging classes don't count as a way of "getting people in the door." Banks don't have the luxury of having "cool" products that drive flocks of people to line up at the door.

Consumer research I've done suggests that people are increasingly engaged with their financial lives. Younger consumers are more engaged with their financial lives than older consumers, and certainly are more so than older consumers were when they were in their 20s and early 30s.

But the financial services industry has a long way to go before it can talk about branches as a place that fosters a sense of "ownership, belonging, and loyalty."

On the Other Hand: In Defense of Bank Branches

A CNBC article on bank branches reported that:[30]

"Mobile transactions are easier for customers and cheaper for banks to service, according to Diebold, a company which specializes in ATM and branch transaction services. In the company's 2010 investor presentation, it estimated a US$4.25 per transaction expense at a bank branch versus only 8 cents through mobile banking. A 2013 Deloitte study found 40 percent of consumers were willing to pay more for the ease of mobile banking, too."

My take: There's a lot wrong with this paragraph. Why would mobile transactions be "easier" for customers? Because they don't have to go to into a branch to conduct the transaction? What if the transaction (or interaction) requires some discussion or involves some level of complexity?

If we're talking about checking the balance on a account, or transferring funds between accounts, then sure, a mobile transaction may be easier for a customer to do than using other channels or through other methods. But the unqualified statement "mobile transactions are easier for customers" doesn't hold water. Unless, of course, you assume that the only transactions that exist are those that are more easily done through a mobile device.

The implication of the second sentence—which states that branch transactions cost an average of US$4.25 per transaction vs. US$0.08 per transaction for mobile transactions—is that shifting transaction volume out of branches and into the mobile channel will result in huge cost savings for banks and credit unions.

Won't happen. Not unless you shut down a large number of branches, which is a whole lot easier said than done. In addition, these cost estimates are terribly misleading. They are not variable costs. The branch does not start the day with US$0.00 in costs and add US$4.25 (on average) every time someone comes in to conduct a transaction.

The CNBC article quotes Brett King as saying "Customers, on average, visit a branch 85% less than they did in 1995." Assuming that the branch transaction volume declined by

85%, then a driver of the supposedly high transaction costs in a branch is the fact that the volume of transactions is insufficient relative to the cost of operating the channel.

And if you do shut down branches, there might be negative side effects. Again, from the CNBC article:

> "Even in the face of real estate and transaction costs, bank branches are a critical tool to attract new customers—if only serving as expensive billboards for the company in a choice-heavy world. "It's going to be very difficult to convince people…that you're a major presence in a market and you're here to serve them if you don't have any physical presence," said Jonathan Larsen, Citigroup's global head of retail banking."

This really gets to the problem of the channel costs that people throw around. The US$0.08 mobile channel transaction likely produces no revenue, while the US$4.25 transaction might.

It's akin to why I want to slap people who think direct mail is dead upside their heads. It's about ROI. If a <1% response rate produces $1 million in revenue for a $10k investment in direct mail, and a 10% response rate in another channel (e.g., social media) produces $10k in revenue for a $1k investment, the larger response rate doesn't matter. Sure, the social media campaign cost less, but the direct mail campaign produced more revenue.

It's the same with channel costs. Looking at average transaction costs ignores the composition of those transactions. Smart managers don't ignore the transaction composition.

My guess is that Apple could save a lot of money by cramming its products into much smaller stores, and locate those stores in the seedy sections of the cities where they do business. In fact, they could just shut down those stores, and take all product orders online. I'm sure the company could develop a mobile app to merchandise products and take orders.

Yet it doesn't, and everybody with a Twitter account falls over each other to tell the world how great their Apple store experience was.

Nobody brags about their bank branch experiences, though (except for my dad).

The real problem with bank branches isn't a higher cost per transaction. It's a two-fold problem: 1) transaction composition is (still) skewed too much towards service (vs. sales) transactions, and 2) those sales transactions suck.

OK, that last point (#2) was unfair and unsubstantiated.

But the fact of the matter is that many of the sales-related transactions that occur in branches are conducted by employees unqualified to help consumers make smart decisions about their financial lives. And the information that the employers—banks and credit unions—provide to those employees to help conduct those sales transactions is woefully lacking.

There are industry participants and observers who think that branches will become places where consumers will go to discuss their financial needs and lives, and become more sales-oriented than service-oriented. Others think branches are dead (or rapidly dying) and have no shortage of data to prove their point.

This is a stupid debate. There is no reason why any particular bank or credit union couldn't go branchless. And there's no reason why any particular bank couldn't make its branches the equivalent of an Apple store.

It's not a matter of whether or not branches are a good idea (or not), or whether they're alive or dead. It's a matter of execution, and being committed to making the branch work (or getting rid of them), and understanding the inconsistent and conflicting decisions that so many banks make that undermine channel strategies.

What To Do With Bank Branches

While I would be perfectly happy to see branches go away, that's not likely, nor realistic. There are some interactions that simply still have to be done in a branch.

Recently, I needed to cash in some savings bonds. Maybe remote deposit capture was a possibility there, but I don't think so. I guess I could have put the savings bonds in an envelope and mailed them into the bank, but while I'm not the brightest bulb on the planet, I wasn't stupid enough to do that. I'm nitpicking, of course. It's possible to use a smartphone to scan those bonds and avoid the branch. But there are other things that involve the use of a branch that are harder to replace.

Reality: As long as there are still physical (versus digital) elements to the world of banking, there will be a need for branches.

The "preferences" argument is totally laughable. Asking consumers what channels they "prefer" and then using those "preferences" to proclaim the death or future of the branch is just bad research.

Point #1: Consumers will use whatever mechanism is most convenient to them at the moment they want to do something.

Point #2: Sometimes consumers "prefer" to do something in one channel versus another, not because the interaction is so great in that preferred channel, but because it sucks so bad in the non-preferred channel. Translation: Maybe applying for loans online would be preferred by more consumers if the process were better.

Reality: Consumers' stated preferences (at a point in time) are lousy indicators of a channel's future viability.

The branch evolution discussion—which usually comes down to proclamations about how the branch will evolve to one that involves mostly sales interactions—typically omits any details on how this transformation or evolution is going to come about.

If branches aren't where consumers go for sales-related discussions today, why would things be any different in the future?

Consumers channel behavior regarding sales interactions follow generation-dominated trends: Seniors use the branches, Boomers use the phone, and Gen Xers and Yers use.....well, I'm not quite sure what they use. I'm inclined to believe that Gen Yers haven't had many sales-related interactions to discern any trends in channel use.

So, if the pundits think that the branch of the future is going to be a place where consumers go to sit and discuss their financial lives with well-trained branch reps, then a lot of things have to change. Not just with the design of branches and the staffing of employees within the branch, but in the minds of consumers.

In other words, it's going to take a lot of marketing effort to educate and persuade customers (those of the future, that is) to use bank branches for these perceived purposes.

Bottom line: It's ironic. When the online channel was emerging, smart banks realized that they had to "market" the channel to drive customer utilization. Who would've thought the pendulum would have swung so far that they now have to market the branches to drive usage?

Distorted Visions of the Bank of the Future

An American Banker article titled *Conestoga Takes Branch Video to the Next Level* starts off by saying:[31]

"Richard Elko excitedly describes the reinvention of consumer banking at Conestoga Bank, a path toward branches that more closely resemble small, virtualized pieces of the central office than separate outposts. "We wake up in the morning and say 'what should a bank look like in today's world?' If Google or Apple had a bank, what would it look like?," says the CEO of the $622 million Chester Springs, Pa.-based Conestoga."

I assume that what Mr. Elko is asking is "if Apple had a bank, what would its branches look like?"

The focus on "how Google or Apple would run a bank" is misplaced. Apple sells technology products. Products that people can interact with, and that they like to interact with before buying them. I'm sure I'm not alone in my behavior: When I go to the mall with the wife and kids, they go into 50 different stores looking at clothing, shoes, and make up. I go to the Apple store and play with the products.

Show me the guy who goes to the mall and hangs out at the bank branch while the wife and kids are spending all his money, and I'll show you a bank robber. (Casing the joint is probably a good use of time for a would-be bank robber, no?).

I can't imagine that Apple—if it owned or started a bank— would build bank branches that only provided banking services. I also can't imagine that Apple would dedicate more than two or three square feet of its existing retail locations to banking services.

Recent reports suggest that Apple's store employees earn about $12 per hour, on average, and generate $500k in sales per employee.

Good luck to Mr. Elko trying to replicate those numbers.

Conestoga's approach to the branch design challenge is "video and file transfer techniques to allow more robust video-enabled transactions, including the commencement of new credit and savings products; in effect adding video sales to earlier video teller services."

I've made some rough estimates, and I'm not convinced the economics are favorable.

To build this model, I'm guessing that it'll cost $500k to implement video-based services in a 25-branch bank.

Another key element of the model is the sales productivity of the branch. To make this estimate, I used the average number of retail checking accounts opened per branch (16.9) that Cornerstone Advisors estimated (and reported on Bankstocks. com). Cornerstone also found that accounts opened per branch in 2010 was down 10% from 2007. The model contains four scenarios (Table 6.1):

Table 6.1

	Baseline	Scenario 1	Scenario 2	Scenario 3	Scenario 4
# of branches	25	25	25	25	25
Technology investment	$500,000				
Sales-related branch visits per month	100	100	97	97	103
Sales effectiveness ratio	16.9%	18.6%	18.6%	20.3%	18,6%
Checking accounts opened per branch per month	16.9	18.6	18.0	19.7	19.1
Annual revenue per checking account	$100	$100	$100	$100	$100
Total revenue	$507,000	$557,000	$540,969	$590,148	$574,431
Five-year ROI		31%	34%	53%	57%
Payback period (years)		10	15	6	7

Source: Author

Scenario 1. In the first scenario, I assume that the implementation of video sales capabilities improves sales productivity by 10%, and I assume away the downward decline in account openings per branch. The five-year ROI of this scenario is 51%, with a 10-year payback period.

Scenario 2. In the second scenario, I add in the 3% downward trend in account openings with the assumption that it doesn't represent a decline in sales effectiveness, but instead, a decline in the number of overall branch visits. This reduces the five-year ROI to 34%, with a 15-year payback period.

Scenario 3. In the third scenario, I upped the estimate for sales effectiveness improvement from 10% to 20%, and kept the 3% downward trend in overall branch visits. The five-year ROI improves to 83%, and reduces the payback period to 6 years.

Scenario 4. In the fourth scenario, I went back to the 10% effectiveness gain, but made an assumption that implementing video sales could help drive traffic into the branches, and introduced a 3% annual gain in monthly branch visits. The result: A five-year ROI of 67%, and a payback period of seven years.

Clearly, the ROI of this branch of the future vision is dependent on some rough estimates I've made here. If the cost of implementation is $250k instead of $500k, you can double the ROI numbers, and cut the payback period in half.

But there's another element here that shouldn't be overlooked: These estimates implicitly assume that any increase in branch sales effectiveness is entirely due to the implementation of video sales capabilities.

In other words, it assumes—in the language of economists—"all other things being equal." But all "other things" are never equal. Banks will continue to advertise, and make investments in other marketing technologies and tactics will make it difficult to attribute the results of an increase in branch traffic and branch sales effectiveness to a single investment.

Bottom line: Even if banks could lure people back into bank branches, the improvement in sales effectiveness needed to make the investment profitable would be substantial. The 5-year ROI estimates in my model just don't cut it. (Feel free to shoot holes in my model—I know it's based on some rough estimates).

But proponents of the vision that bank branches are going to metamorphose into high-tech sales centers—where consumers come in to discuss their financial lives with Max Headroom on a TV monitor—need to rethink that vision, or back up their visions with some economic reasoning.

In fact, it may be just as likely that the future role of the branch is strictly service—and not sales—related. That the branch will be the place where people go to get the sticky problems fixed.

What Apple (and car dealers, for that matter) teaches us is that when you have a product that people can touch—and want to touch—before buying, having physical locations that show off those products are good investments. Financial services are different.

Would You Prefer a Relationship With a Ton of Bricks?

Vernon Hill, former CEO of Commerce Bank, once wrote:

> "The bank branch is the cornerstone, not the millstone, of retail banking. The point of a bank branch is to reflect your brand and to open new relationships. How do you build a relationship with a machine?"

My take: Hill is wrong about the power of the Internet to build relationships, and misinterprets the nature of what contributes to building a customer relationship.

Commerce's branch-centric strategy has a short half-life to it. The future of retail banking isn't represented by aging boomers and seniors looking for mid-morning chats with the assistant manager of their local bank branch.

The future of retail banking lies in the provision of good, objective advice and guidance on managing one's finances, and the fast and flawless delivery of transactions and services.

The reality is that a "machine"—i.e., the Internet or a remote capture device—can often do this as well, if not better, than somebody in a branch or a call center (increasingly located in some far away land).

If it isn't possible to develop a relationship with a "machine", then how do you account for the success of Amazon.com? Don't tell me, "oh, that's different—it isn't financial services." That argument doesn't fly. Consumers don't care—to them it's just another type of product or service in which they're looking for help in making the right decision, and a fast and painless way to get that product or service.

So how does Amazon succeed at building relationships using only a machine as a contact point? Interestingly, the answer lies in one of Hill's own statements.

Hill says that "the point of a bank branch is to reflect your brand." But what really is a bank branch? Answer: Nothing but a ton of bricks. The people within that branch come and go over time, and many customers never learn the names of those people anyway. But it's the nature of how interactions are handled within that branch that lead customers to form an opinion about the bank.

In other words, the branch becomes the "face" of the bank in the eyes of the customer. And please listen, Mr. Hill, because increasingly, the Internet is the face of banks for many customers, especially those under the age of 40.

This doesn't mean, as I've written before, that branches go away. Until banks build out all the service functionality that's available in the branch on their Web sites, that won't happen. Bank branches are security blankets.

Hill is right that customers don't want a relationship with a machine. But they don't want a relationship with a ton of bricks either. It's what that machine or ton of bricks represents in the mind of the customer that matters. And that perception is formed more by the quality of the interactions that occur.

Bottom line: Relationship value is assigned to the quality of the interaction, not the location where that interaction took place.

Earlier in the book, I quoted psychologist John Gottman who said that relationships are about the small moments of attachment and intimacy. It doesn't matter where those moments occur.

If a bank customer who considers convenience to be an important driver of their bank relationship uses a remote capture device and consciously thinks about the convenience that the device provides—then a step towards strengthening that relationship has occurred.

The Challenges in Making Bank Branch Decisions

Banks with an existing branch network must address two strategic questions regarding their branches:

1) What is the cost of acquisition (not delivery) that established banks have to incur with a cost structure that includes branches?

   The question banks must address isn't "Do we need branches?" but "How do we attack the cost structure to more profitably deliver services?"

   If the effectiveness of a bank's customer acquisition efforts is reduced by reducing or eliminating the branch network, that bank needs to maintain a branch network.

   To answer the question, however requires a reliable set of performance metrics. Which leads us to the next strategic question...

2) What channel-related metrics are needed to make smart decisions about allocating resources to channels?

   A few years ago, a couple of First Manhattan Consulting Group (FMCG) executives wrote, in Bankstocks.com:

"One metric stands out as being highly correlated to growth in a bank's shareholder value: Same-store deposit growth. Banks that consistently generate strong same-store deposit growth in their mature branches tend to generate strong growth in other relevant measures, as well."

I don't doubt FMCG's analysis that the metric is highly correlated with shareholder return and other ROI-oriented metrics. But correlation does not equal causation. The potential pitfall that bank executives face is a myopic focus on a single metric (like the Net Promoter Score), or even too narrow a set of metrics.

Channel-specific metrics hamper managers' ability to effectively understand overall performance and how to allocate—or reallocate—funds across channels and initiatives.

But even if banks were to obtain a reliable set of metrics, they would still have to address a third strategic question...

3) What is the political feasibility of reducing branch presence?

Want to close branches where there is a high concentration of senior citizens? The AARP might get on your case. Want to close branches in poor, urban areas? Consumer advocate groups will be in your face. Want to close branches in affluent suburbs? Wait, why would you want to do that?

Established banks may not be able to significantly reduce their branch presence.

Humor Break
The Branch of the Future

Back in the 1950s, Deutsche Bank commissioned an artist to envision the "branch of the future." Apparently, in the future, bank branches will consist of little more than holographic obelisks, and women in bathing suits will fly through the air to get to bank branches.

And now you know why I will continue to go to bank branches whenever I can.☺

Source: Deutsche Bank

PART III
THE NEW CONSUMERS

Chapter Seven
Debunking the Myths
About Gen Y

There seems to be a desire among some people—perhaps even Gen Yers themselves—to paint Gen Y (people born between 1978 and 1994) as a generation that isn't motivated by that evil thing called money, that is mistrustful of those evil people called bankers, and that isn't enticed by that evil product called a credit card.

It's time to debunk a few myths regarding this generation's attitudes towards money and financial services need some closer scrutiny.

Myth #1: Gen Yers Aren't Motivated by Money

Myth: Insight Magazine claimed that "for Gen Y, money isn't the be-all and end-all," the Brazen Careerist wrote "Gen Y is not motivated by money...unless they're in Sales," and for good measure I found another blogger who reports that "in my experience, Gen Y is not motivated by money."

Reality: Gen Yers are no less motivated by money than anybody else. First off, every generation has its share of people who are highly motivated by money, and those who are less motivated by money. The views stated above—as I read them—are trying to imply that on the whole (i.e., a higher percentage of), Gen Yers are less motivated by money than members of other generations.

Hogwash. In research conducted by Aite Group, six in ten Gen Yers said that money is as important to them as it to their parents, and a quarter of respondents said it's more important. Now it's possible, of course, that someone could have said that money is more important to them than it is to their parents—and still not be motivated by money, if their parents are really not motivated by money. But the myth being propagated here is about the relative view of money on the part of Gen Yers—and the data simply doesn't support the myth.

And as for the 15% who said money isn't as important to them as it is to their parents: Just wait a couple of years until they get married, have kids, want to buy a house, a new car, need to save for kids' college education, etc. Then let's see how important money is to them.

Myth #2: Gen Yers Don't Trust Banks

Myth: A study commissioned by Microsoft found that "adults between 18 and 29 years old don't trust traditional financial institutions very much," while Wallet Pop went beyond that to state that Gen Yers "don't trust banks, don't plan to invest in the stock market, and don't even want to get insurance."[32]

Reality: As we discussed in Chapter Three, few people of any age trust banks these days. Actually, to be more specific, a minority of people trust "banks in general." This is an important nuance.

This is particularly true for Gen Yers. In fact, 45% of the Gen Yers surveyed said that they trust banks (in general), in contrast to just 33% of older consumers. So myth debunked right there. This shouldn't be surprising—older consumers have years and years of bad experiences with a lot of the different banks they've done business with. They've earned the right to be mistrustful. How much experience has a 23 year old had with banks in order to be so mistrustful?

But more importantly, about seven in ten Gen Yers said they trust their primary bank, compared to 73% of the older consumers who said the same. Not a big gap there. And that's the type of trust that matters most—trust in the bank they do business with, not trust with some amorphous definition of banks in general.

Myth #3: Gen Yers Don't Want Credit Cards

Myth: At a conference I recently attended, one of the speakers said "credit cards will become obsolete—Gen Yers will never adopt them." US News and World Report, reporting on a book called Not Quite Adults, says the authors of the book found that Gen Yers "meticulously avoid credit card debt."

Reality: Nonsense. Nearly six in 10 "young" Gen Yers— those born between 1987 and 1993—owned a credit card in 2013, up from 32% in 2008. Among "old" Gen Yers—those born between 1978 and 1986—76% had a credit card in 2013, a jump of nine percentage points over 2008.33

Furthermore, "meticulously avoiding credit card debt" is not the same as not wanting or needing credit cards. Personally, I avoid credit card debt as well (hey! I must be a Gen Yer! NOT). And I use a credit card for nearly every purchase I make. The reason Gen Yers are less likely to use credit cards has nothing to do with some innate attitudinal difference. The answer is much simpler: They simply haven't got to the point in their lives where they need as many credit cards as older consumers do.

When Gen Yers who don't have a credit card were asked why they don't have one, the most popular answer was "never had the need, but I anticipate applying for one in the future." The second most popular answer was "no reason."

Myth #4: Gen Yers Don't Use Bank Branches

Myth: I came across a blog post recently that contained the following passage:

> "My boss Gordon told me an interesting story. His 22-year-old son was having an issue with his bank, and didn't know how to solve the problem. Gordon said, "Well, if you're not getting an answer online, why don't you drive over to the bank branch and talk to someone in person?" His son didn't know where his bank was located—and didn't even realize the bank even had physical locations. This response is very representative of Gen Y."

Reading this, I couldn't help but wonder if Gordon's son knew that he could use his smartphone—which is what he might have been using to access his bank account online—to actually CALL the bank and talk to someone. It's a real shame that some Gen Yers are using so little of the capabilities that their smartphones offer.

Although the view that Gen Yers don't know about bank branches may not be widespread, there are other pieces of evidence pointing to the view that members of this generation don't use the branches.

A 30-year-old VP of Marketing at a $47 million in assets, 8,135-member credit union was quoted in Credit Union Management magazine as saying "We (Gen Yers) don't want to drive to the branch or even talk to an actual human being if we don't have to." The LemmonTree Marketing Group discovered in its research that Gen Yers "are less likely [than members of other generations] to ever enter a bank branch and want to do all their banking on their own schedule from home."[34]

Reality: From conducting market research over the years, I have come to this conclusion: For every research study you find to support a point, there are two studies that refute it.

Financial technology company Fiserv surveyed consumers and found that:

"Gen Yers do not limit themselves to online and mobile banking—they're more likely than any other age segment to visit a branch, drive up to an ATM or phone a call center.

For each of the banking services above, Gen Y represents the highest percentage of high volume users (five or more visits/uses per month) than any other age segment. The survey found that 17% of Gen Y members visited a branch or office five or more times in the past month, compared with Gen X's 10%, Baby Boomers' 10% and Seniors' 11%. High volume users of ATMs equaled 34% of Gen Y respondents, 30% of Gen X respondents, 22% of Baby Boomer respondents and 12% of Senior respondents. 6% of Gen Y members are high volume users of call centers, compared with Gen X's 2%, Baby Boomers' 1% and Seniors' 0%."

Not only do Gen Yers still use bank branches, they're not even the generation most likely to open accounts online. When consumers shopping for checking accounts were asked about the likelihood of them opening the account online, just three in 10 consumers under the age of 30 said that they anticipated applying online. That's in contrast to 41% of those in their 30s and 33% of consumers in their 40s.

According to Rob Rubin, Managing Director of consulting firm Novarica, and founder of FindABetterBank.com:[35]

"Consumers are only comfortable purchasing products or services online that they completely understand. And the reality is that many younger consumers shopping online for banking products have little-to-no experience with banking products. A survey among checking account shoppers on FindABetterBank found that those under 30 were 30% more likely to say they didn't have a checking account. It is this lack of experience that pushes many Gen-Y consumers into branches to open accounts."

Bottom line: The romanticized view of Gen Yers is simply not a realistic one. Reality:

1) Money is important to all of this. More important to some than others, for sure, but that difference is not generational-based. Money is always going to be more important to someone starting or supporting a family than someone who isn't.

2) Trust is a tricky thing to measure. For the past few years, banks have been our whipping boys for the sorry state of the economy and financial crisis. It isn't a generational thing.

3) As Gen Yers age, their financial needs will evolve, their credit scores will improve, and their demand for credit—and credit cards—will rise. That doesn't mean their credit card debt will rise to the level that previous generations took it to, but there will be demand for credit.

4) And if the bank branch really is a dying concept, it isn't because of Gen Yers.

The REAL Gen Y Difference: The Venmo Line

The folks over at quartz.com published an article which recounted an internal online conversation various staff members had one morning regarding online P2P payments (in particular, Venmo).[36] The article reporting the exchange distinguished between the over-30 year olds at Quartz, and those under the age of 30.

You can probably guess what the comments from the over-30 group were:

"Seriously, do enough people pay enough other people with enough frequency to support all these person-to-person payment apps? Haven't people ever heard of splitting a bill?"

"Why on earth would anyone care what their friends are paying each other?"

So why would those "crazy kids" use this technology?

"Venmo is great also because it is sort of a social network too, like you have to put in a sort of "memo" field and so you see a news feed of what your friends paid each other for"

"Because people write funny things....with emoji usually"

Not that I have any clue (as a way-over-30 year old) what "emoji" is. The folks at Quartz called this generational split the Venmo Line.

My take: The Venmo Line is the essence of how Gen Yers are truly different from older generations.

I'm tired of hearing Gen Yers describe themselves as social. That's not how they're different. Once upon a time, I was young, free, and single (or more accurately, childless)–and, as a result, social. Believe it or not, there once was a time when Baby Boomers went out at 10:30 pm–and not, like now, to bed. Gen Yers might have a hard time believing this, but previous generations were just as social as Gen Yers think they are. What previous generations had, that Gen Yers apparently don't, however, are boundaries.

Older generations didn't (and don't) share personal financial information. We don't share a lot of personal information that Gen Yers seemingly have no problem sharing with everyone else. That doesn't make the social, or more social. It simply makes them...different.

That's the Venmo line: What you have no qualms about sharing and what you do have qualms about.

There is another important aspect to The Venmo Line. It has to do with why they use Venmo in the first place.

One of the "elders" at Quartz (who is probably no older than 35) asked: "Do enough people pay enough other people with enough frequency to support all these person-to-person payment apps?"

The answer is YES! I've sized P2P payments (all of them, not just online) in the US, and the answer is that P2P payments total nearly $1 trillion (which is only about a quarter of retail sales or monthly bill pay).

This volume isn't lost on banks, who for years have been touting their online P2P payment capabilities (through capabilities like CashEdge) without much success.

But along comes Venmo, and adoption among the under-30 crowd is widespread (Sadly, I have no data to prove that. My contention comes from input from my older daughter who says all her friends use Venmo, and from Drew Sievers, who says that all the young people who live in that outlier of a bubble in the universe called Silicon Valley use it).

The question is, why have they adopted Venmo when banks have had this capability for a long time?

The "coolness" factor. It's cool to use Venmo. It's not cool to use anything from a bank. This is another view of the Venmo Line: People "below" the line (the under 30 crowd) will adopt a particular vendor's technology if it's perceived as cool, even if there are a million other providers of that technology.

Those of us "above" the line may use that technology–and others like Twitter and Facebook, and whatever–but we're a lot less likely to do so because it's "cool."

Credit Unions' Average Age Of Member Obsession

For a few years now, credit unions have been obsessed (not too strong a word) with reducing the average age of their member base.

The rationale goes something like this: Younger consumers represent the future of credit unions, therefore we have to attract more Gen Yers and reduce the average age of our members.

My take: OK, I can see some logic in this. But it doesn't make mathematical sense.

Allow me to explain this with some examples. Imagine, for simplicity sake, that your credit union has 100 members, all of whom turn 47 sometime during 2013, and that each member produces a strong $10 in profit.

2013 Average age of members: 47. Total profits: $1000. Average profits per member: $10.

Now consider the following scenarios:

Scenario A. In this scenario, the credit union enjoys 100% member retention going into 2014, with no change in member profitability. But no new member growth.

2014 average age of members: 48. Total profits: $1000. Average profits per member: $10.

Oh no! The average age of member went up! This is terrible!

Well, not really. The lack of new member growth isn't good, but maintaining good profits and profitability levels is nothing to sneeze at. And, after all, many marketing gurus think you should be focused on marketing to existing members since somehow they think that's less expensive.

Scenario B. In this scenario, your credit union brings in 10 new members, each of whom is 25 years old, and who each produce $5 of profits. But your credit union loses six existing members.

On the face of it, this doesn't sound too bad. 5% new member growth is pretty good in the scheme of things, as is 94% retention.

2014 average age of members: 46. Total profits: $990. Average profits per member: $9.52.

You succeeded in lowering the average age of your members from 47 to 46. Hooray for you! You also reduced the overall profits by 1%, however, and average profitability per member by nearly 5%. Not so good. I don't think there's a credit union in this country that doesn't boast about how it's member-owned, and how everything it does is for the benefit of the members. If that's so, can you explain to me how intentionally reducing the overall profitability of the organization—and hence, member dividends—is beneficial to existing members?

A speaker at a conference that I attended claimed that "the average age of credit union members grows by 2 years, every 5 years." I don't know the source of that statistic, but I did find this, written by Paul Gentile of CUNA in October 2012:[37]

> "The average age of a credit union member is 47 years old. That average has been going up, not down, over the years. Back in 1989 it was 42.8 and in 2000 it was 44.7."

Let's do a little math here, shall we?

What Gentile is saying is that the average age of credit union members grows by two years roughly every 10, not five years. Between 1989 and 2012—a 23 year time period—the average age of credit union members only grew by four years.
In other words, over a 23 year time period, while your members themselves aged by 23 years (this is a law of nature, unless you belong to the Dorian Gray Credit Union), the average age of credit union members only grew by four years.

What's wrong with credit union people? Did they not pass third-grade arithmetic class?

Bottom line: With a high member retention rate, the vast majority of your members stay with you year to year. Their age increases by one every year. The fact that the average age of the credit union member base increases by two years for every 10 years that have elapsed is a sign of amazing success in acquiring younger members.

Humor Break
Redefining the Generations

There's way too much discussion about the generations, what characteristics define the generations, and who belongs to which generation.

That's why I've come up with a new generation classification scheme:

1. **Gen What?** Gen What-ers are generally clueless about what's going on in the world. Don't use the terms "social media" or "blog" in front of a Gen What-er—you're likely to become frustrated. Partially because, well let's face it—at their age, their hearing is starting to fail, and they'll simply keep responding "what?" to everything you say. I hope I didn't offend any of them, but the reality is that none of them read books anymore, so they won't see this in the first place.

2. **Gen Wine.** Gen Winers—sometimes referred to as Baby Boomers—is the generation responsible for displacing beer as the alcoholic drink of choice. You can always tell who's the Gen Winer at the dinner table. We're the ones who think we (oops, I mean "they") know everything about wine—which is the best with what food, which wineries are the best to visit when you go to Napa, which years are the best, etc. Unfortunately, this arrogant, snobby, omniscient

attitude creeps into pretty much every other aspect of Gen Winers' lives. Can you say "insufferable bore"?

3. **Gen Whine.** It wasn't until recently that I learned what the term emo meant. Gen Whiners define emo. The fact that a lot of people who are referred to as Gen Xers are also Gen Whiners could simply be coincidental. Everything—and I mean everything—that happens in the world has a deep, scarring, and emotional impact on Gen Whiners' lives. And unfortunately, they feel the need to tell the rest of us about it.

4. **Gen Wired.** The label has nothing to do with their proclivity to be on the Internet 20 hours a day, conversing on the 37 social networks that they belong to. No, it refers to their caffeine addiction. Twice daily trips to Starbucks is nothing unusual for Gen Wired. They know what everything on the Starbucks' menu means. And most annoyingly, they have to tweet about every stop they make at Starbucks, and let the rest of us know what they ordered.

These are the "new" generations, and here's the beauty of my generation classification scheme: It doesn't matter which year you're born in. You get to choose your generation!

So, no more agonizing over whether or not you're part of one generation or another just because you were born in, say, 1979. The fact that you even thought about it in the first place makes you a Gen Whiner.

Chapter Eight
The Real Underserved Market: Gen Why

An article titled The Credit Union World Attracting Gen Y to Ensure Its Bright Future contains the following passage:[38]

> "Every day since January 1, 2011, more than 10,000 Baby Boomers reach age 65, and that is going to continue every single day for the next 19 years. That adds up to about 64 million skilled workers who will be able to retire in the near future. What does this mean for the American workforce and nearly every business, large and small? The future of the workforce will depend on the next generation of young workers and professionals—Gen Y. Credit unions must learn to successfully market to Gen Y in order to attract and retain them, and ultimately ensure their own existence and growth."

My take: Don't believe this. I'm not disputing the Boomer numbers. Yes, (on average) 10,000 boomers reach the age of 65 every day. Out of 77 million boomers, however, 10,000 is a pretty small number. What I am disputing is this: "That adds up to about 64 million skilled workers who will be able to retire in the near future."

Reality: Many boomers—I can't quantify it—will not be able to, or will choose not to retire in the near future.

Are there really people out there who cling to the out-dated notion that on people's 65th birthday, they go into work, get their gold watch, eat a piece of cake at their going-away party, then go home to pack up the house for the move to Florida the next day?

What this really means for "nearly every business or company" is that older employees will be sticking around a whole lot longer than they did in the past. And what this really means for banks goes beyond having to "learn to successfully market to Gen Y in order to attract and retain them."

Compared to older consumers, Gen Yers are more likely to do household budgeting, to categorize and forecast their expenses, and to seek out advice on how to make better financial decisions. Even though they're only in their 20s (or maybe early 30s), many are already concerned about, and saving for retirement.

People over the age of 65 are the least likely to budget, to categorize and forecast their expenses, to access financial education material, and to analyze the allocation of their investments.

Is that because they already have this stuff nailed down, and it's no longer a problem or issue to manage their financial lives because they're swimming in dough, and don't have to worry about it on a day-to-day basis? Yeah, sure.

The real underserved market in banking isn't Gen Y—it's Gen WHY: Gen We Haven't-stopped-working Yet. What Gen WHY needs is help managing their financial lives: Understanding how much they'll need in retirement, how to manage their money in retirement, how to pass down their money after their retirement is over.

But the banking industry doesn't have a product for that. Financial advisors (some of whom work for banks or credit unions) can provide a service to fill that need.

But many people have never paid for financial advice. They're used to paying for financial products: A checking account, a savings account, a CD, etc. And what banks and credit unions have learned to do (in varying degrees of effectiveness) is sell financial products, not financial services.

Bottom line: 1) The bigger short-term opportunity presented by the 10k of boomers who reach 65 every day is not selling to Gen Yers, but providing better support and help to those boomers who aren't retiring, can't retire, but might want to; and 2) The real challenge to the industry is not "learning how to market to Gen Yers," but how to transition from selling financial products to financial services.

Chapter Nine
Moms: The Real
Decision-Makers

According to a study by the Boston Consulting Group (BCG), in 59% of US households, the female head of household is in charge of the family's finances.[39] As a man with the $7 in my pocket that my wife lets me out of the house with, I can attest to this trend.

The BCG statistic leads pundits to conclude that banks should target women, and do a better job of marketing to them. But there is one problem here: You can't market financial services to "women".

Before you jump to conclusions—and all over my head—read first, and then let me have it if you're so inclined.

There's renewed talk these days in financial services circles about marketing to women. Renewed, because at the height of the dot-com boom, start-ups like the Women's Financial Network emerged, dedicated to providing financial services to women.

More recently, a CU Times article titled *Marketing to Woman Require Cultural Change* asserted that the reason why many credit unions' marketing programs don't directly speak to women is that:[40]

"The majority of the industry's leadership are still primarily male...and most males are unable to transfer facts to actions when challenged to focus their attention on the growing power of women, both in the marketplace as well as the workplace."

On her Marketing To Women blog, marketing expert Holly Buchanan encouraged credit unions interested in marketing to women to (among other things): 1) Make them feel smart; 2) Use female-friendly language; 3) Create kid-friendly branches; and 4) Support her causes.[41]

My take: Marketing financial services products to "women" is doomed to fail, and simply not a very good idea. [Put the pins down, and keep reading before you stab your Ron Shevlin voodoo doll].

In her post, Holly quotes a source that says women make 89% of the banking decisions for their families (BCG says 59% of household finances are managed by women, but I guess it's possible that they could make 89% of the decisions).

But, if 89% of the decisions are made by women, then pretty much all of the decisions are made by women, no? Which means, the only people worth marketing to are women.

But let me ask you marketers something: Imagine for a moment that there was no way for you to know the gender of your customers and prospects. How would you segment consumers in order to learn their needs, attitudes, and preferences, as they pertain to the products they buy and how they buy them?

You would look at age, income, life stage, channel preferences, etc., right?

If you did that you might find differences in behaviors and preferences between Gen Yers and Boomers, or differences between low income and high income consumers, or differences between people with young children and those (even of similar age and income) who don't have children.

You would then use the segments you identified to learn how to best design products and marketing campaigns to reach consumers within each of those segments.

After doing all of the above, if I then came back and told you that all of your customers and prospects were of just one gender, what would you change? Answer: Nothing! You would have already learned what the real drivers of different needs and preferences were.

What I'm trying to convey here—but worried that I'm not articulating clearly—is that "women" is not a manageable, marketable consumer segment. It's way too broad (oh geez, no pun intended).

In the history of consumer products, many companies have successfully sold feminine (or female-oriented) products via male product managers. Marketing is about learning about consumer needs, designing products to meet those needs, and implementing marketing programs that reach and influence the target market(s).

Should Fisher-Price fire everybody over the age of six because they're not the primary users and audience for the products (toys) they produce?

Of course not.

The Right Way to Market to Women

Verity Credit Union is a US$397 million credit union based in Seattle, WA. Verity's target market: Moms.

While the overall market of Moms is pretty large, Verity focuses its marketing efforts on women in the their late 20s (at the younger end) to the early 40s (at the older end). In other words, mostly Gen Xers who are hitting the prime of their earning years, and the prime of their financial needs.

Verity did this, by the way, without firing the entire leadership staff, and replacing them with Moms.

What the credit union did do, was hire a Mom to blog, tweet, and be the "face" of Verity to this market segment. While certainly filling an important role, this person is hardly a senior manager in the organization.

Verity's former chief marketing officer, Shari Storm, describes the credit union's approach:[42]

"Verity did a number of things to reach the Mom market:

1. **Created family-friendly branches.** We wanted kids to love visiting the credit union. We wanted to win the hearts and minds of kids long before they became teenagers. To that end, we built children's corners, had a multitude of giveaways and contests. Santa comes, the Easter Bunny comes, we build huge statues out of Peeps in the spring, we periodically have cookies and hot cocoa on cold days. We are always the place that gives out stickers, suckers, coins, anything to make kids love visiting the credit union.

2. **Renamed our checking account to Cartwheel Checking.** Verity's creative centers around parents watching their kids play, the sound of children laughing, radio spots that say things like, "remember when the toughest thing you had to worry about was perfecting your cartwheel" (cue to sound of children laughing).

3. **Focused on providing convenience services.** Services like mobile, mobile deposit capture and PFM became more important to us because we understood how critical easy-to-use services are to this demographic."

What makes Moms such a good market to sell to? According to Storm:

"There are reasons beyond Mom's spending power that make them a smart target market. The most important is their influence over their families. Parents are the number one indicator of where their children will do their banking. A study by The Money Advice Service asked more than

1,000 teenagers about their financial habits. When it comes to taking advice on money matters, 15 to 17 year olds have a clear hierarchy of who they turn to. More than three quarters (77%) of those surveyed said they find their parents' financial advice most helpful. I have long contended that financial institutions' focus on teens and consumers in their early twenties is misguided. By the time a consumer is in their teens, they have made their banking decisions. FIs that want to earn the business of teens must win their business when they are in elementary school.

Another reason Moms make such a good target market is their online behavior. Moms were one of the first groups to embrace blogging, Facebook, Pinterest and Instagram. The blogosphere is inundated with Mom blogs. According to a 2012 Mashable article, there are 3.9 million mom bloggers in the US. Moms congregate online. That is nice for a marketer, because you know where to find Moms. But what makes it good for a strategist is how Moms use social media forums. Moms actively ask for, give and act on referrals. If you want to see this in action, go to Facebook, type in your town's name plus the word Moms and see how many groups come up and how many people belong to those groups."

Why does the credit union's Verity Mom campaign work?

1) **It's grounded in strategy.** It's no big secret that women manage the finances in a majority of households in the US. Yet, how many financial institutions have really overhauled their efforts to not just market to women, but design products and customer-facing processes to appeal to women? Verity Mom is part of a strategy to attract a segment of customers who represent a good chunk of the demand for financial products.

2) **It's integrated into the core of the business.** So many social media efforts that I hear about appear to be one-off experiments that are designed to "test the waters of social

media" or let the firm check off the "we're attempting to innovate" box.

Not at Verity. The Verity Mom initiative has led to the renaming of the credit union's checking account and the redesign of its branches. In addition, Verity Mom blog posts end up on the credit union's home page, not buried somewhere deep in the site, as it often is at other banks.

3) **It oozes with authenticity.** Plenty of financial institutions have run ad campaigns over the years that purport to show "real people" who share their "stories" about the bank or credit union and how great it is. In the end, I guess we could argue whether or not these attempts are successful at influencing perception, but I'll tell you right now I'll be arguing that they don't. Authenticity is something that takes time to achieve. You can't do it in a single shot, with a single ad campaign.

Bottom line: "Women" is not a viable, realistic consumer segment for financial services firms to market to. There are other attributes and dimensions of the market that better determine how financial services firms should design products, and take those products to market.

You may now load your guns and take your shots at me.

Humor Break
Women are People Too
(Who Knew?)

A marketing firm named Brain Sells (haha) says that "marketers targeting a female audience need to understand the critical difference between men and women."

No disagreement there. But some of the conclusions they came to from their research raises a few eyebrows. Here are a few gems from the study, as reported in Marketing Charts:[43]

1. **Women are people.** You think I'm making this up? According to the article, the firm that released the study said that marketers should be aware that "women are people and have personal feelings and social intentions."

2. **Women have the ability to perceive more than the metric of a product attribute or an instance in time.** Apparently, women "appreciate the underlying pattern (idea) that gives rise to the fleeting moment." Unfortunately, as a guy, I have no idea what this means.

3. **For women, bigger is not necessarily better.** This is a huge relief to me, personally. Enough said.

As a guy with a wife and three daughters, I was hoping to learn something about women here. Guess I'll have to find another study.

Chapter Ten
The Rise of The Smartphonatics

In an article titled *Consumers show cautious interest in Mobile Payments*, Payments Source reported on a study of US consumers' views on mobile payments which found that:[44]

- Consumers are "clearly ready for a change," as 27% of consumers "never" use checks.

- One in three U.S. adults is interested in mobile and Near Field Communication-based payments.

- 83% of respondents cited security as the most important factor affecting their interest in mobile payments.

- 62% of respondents prefer financial institutions to take the lead on new payment methods instead of wireless or Internet companies.

Other studies echo this apparent lack of demand for mobile payment:

- **Harris Interactive:** "Only 5% of Americans have scanned their phone for admission to a movie or as an airline ticket, and 3% have done so to pay for clothing or electronics, admission to a concert, live theater or performance, or to pay for a convenience item such as coffee. Just under half of Americans (47%) say they are comfortable using a mobile scan as an admission ticket to movies, concerts or live theater performances."

- **Radius Global Market Research:** "The majority of Americans remain quite skeptical of smartphone-generated payment solutions and in the near-term are not likely to give up traditional forms of payment. Security tops the list of concerns about mobile payments."

I guess mobile payment providers should just pack up and go home and find some other business to pursue, eh?

My take: Concluding that consumers are "cautious" in their interest in mobile payments is a misinterpretation of the data.

Concluding that consumers are "ready for a change" because one in four never uses checks misses the point: Consumers have already changed. They've shifted their payments behavior away from checks to debit cards, and yes, cash.

Few consumers are interested in Near Field Communication-based payments because to the Average Joe on the street NFC stands for National Football Conference.

Many consumers cite security as the most important factor affecting their interest in mobile payments because they have no idea what it is, how it works, and don't know what other factors should or could be affecting their interest in mobile payments.

A majority of consumers prefer that banks take the lead on new payment methods instead of wireless or Internet companies because they don't know what "take the lead on new payment methods" means.

These findings aren't surprising. The research efforts cited all violate what should be a rule in market research: Don't ask people to imagine a situation, a state of mind, or something that they can't possibly imagine if they have no basis of experience to do so.

When researchers ask consumers about something that doesn't exist for them—like mobile payments—they don't, and actually can't, get a reliable picture of attitudes and future behavior.

The Emerging Source of Demand for Mobile Payments

Demand for mobile payments isn't "cautious." There's a segment of the population that is chomping at the bit to use mobile payments. And there's a segment that couldn't care less—for right now. There are early adopters and later adopters—but "cautious" isn't an appropriate descriptor.

Looking at overall consumer demand for mobile payments misses the small, but growing segment of consumers that is driving the demand—the **Smartphonatics:**

> *Consumers who change their shopping and payment behavior as a result of owning a smartphone.*

Despite the proliferation of smartphones in the US, not everyone who owns one is a Smartphonatic (smart-fa-NAT-ic). But this group is growing, and their buying power is disproportionately higher than their numbers. They're mostly young, and relatively affluent (for their age).

Smartphonatics are consumers who consider mobile payments and money movement to be "very important" and who express an interest in using a mobile phone to replace their payment cards. Across a global sample, nearly one in four consumers fits this description (Figure 10.1).

Figure 10.1

Interest in having mobile phone replace payment cards

		Low	High
Importance of mobile payments and money movement	Very important	4%	Smartphonatics 24%
	Less important	41%	31%

Source: Aite Group

Smartphonatic penetration varies by country, and represents its mobile maturity level. William Gibson once said that the future is already here, it's just unevenly distributed. That describes interest in mobile payments perfectly. The differences in the various countries' Smartphonatic population is a reflection of the evolution of the mobile channel in each country—and not a reflection of innate differences in attitudes and behaviors of the country's citizens.

Demographically speaking, Smartphonatics are relatively young. By generation, 36% of Gen Yers (consumers between the ages of 20 and 31), almost one-third of Gen Xers (ages 32 to 46), 18% of baby boomers (47 to 65), and 6% of seniors (66+) are Smartphonatics.

The differences in mobile payment and banking behavior between Smartphonatics and other consumers are stark. In the past six months, 70% of Smartphonatics have used their mobile device to make a payment and 80% have used their device for banking purposes. In contrast, among other consumers, less than a quarter have made a mobile payment and only one-third have made mobile banking transactions.

Humor Break
Financial Diseases

You probably don't remember the days when pharma ads didn't dominate TV advertising. The biggest impact these ads have had on me is making me aware of conditions I never knew existed. I have long suspected that pharmaceutical companies invented these diseases. Who ever heard of Low T before they advertised it? Personally, I'm sick of these ads (pun intended), and hearing my wife (jokingly?) say to me every time they air, "maybe that's your problem."

But if the ads didn't work, they wouldn't keep airing them. So it got me thinking: Maybe banks need to do this to help sell their products. Here are a few "conditions," that banks could invent:

1. **Low-C.** Do you find yourself without enough money to go out drinking in the days leading up to your next paycheck? You probably suffer from Low-C (low cash). Instead of trying to sell something as distasteful as a "payday loan," banks should offer Low-C Infusions.

2. **Equitile Dysfunction.** If you don't have the financial power to get that new home improvement up, but have a decent amount of equity in your home, you might have equitile dysfunction. Trying to push "home equity loans" is so 1995. Pharma companies offers Staxyn for ED, so why

don't banks offer Stoxyn for financial ED? Tag line could be: Take Stock In Your Home.

3. **Restless ARM Syndrome.** You know that adjustable rate mortgage that's got you worried, because you're afraid that interest rates will rise? A "fixed mortgage" is no way to cure that disease. If pharma companies can offer Requip for restless leg syndrome, then banks can offer Refin for restless ARM syndrome.

Anyway, it's not my job to come up with this stuff. Financial services marketers need to get a little creative here and take a look outside the industry for what's working in the world of marketing.

CHAPTER ELEVEN
THE UNBANKED, DEBANKED, AND NEOBANKS

Kill the Underbanked

It's time to kill the Underbanked. The label, that is, not the people. An American Banker article titled *Reaching the Underbanked? Try Offering Control* claims:[45]

> "The 37 million American adults who are underbanked have a tough time when it comes to basic financial activities such as paying bills. But banks don't have to sit on the sidelines when it comes to the underbanked. There's an opportunity to service this community through banks. Banks like Regions, Key Bank and Wells Fargo let non-customers come into a branch and receive services and transactions at an affordable price, in a way that's good for the customer and the bank. [For example], Regions offers Now banking services for customers and non-customers that include check cashing at bank branches, reloadable prepaid cards, money transfers, and walk-in bill payment."

My take: This represents a misunderstanding of who and what the underbanked are.

In the FDIC's 2011 National Survey of Unbanked and Underbanked Households, published in September 2012, two categories of consumers are defined as follows:[46]

"Unbanked households are those that lack any kind of deposit account at an insured depository institution. Underbanked households hold a bank account, but also rely on alternative financial services (AFS) providers."

Did you see the second sentence? Underbanked households "hold a bank account." Banks aren't "on the sidelines" when it comes to the underbanked.

When a bank like Regions offers check cashing at its branches to non-customers, it is providing what the FDIC considers to be an alternative financial service (AFS). If you use that service—regardless of whether or not you have a banking account—you're in the Underbanked category. Even though you used that service at a bank!

If that makes sense to you, you belong in Washington, DC.

The term Underbanked has a stigma attached to it, conjuring up the image of someone pushing a stolen grocery shopping cart with all their earthly possessions around town. And that the growing number of them is some kind of epidemic plaguing the nation.

This is total nonsense. You qualify as Underbanked if you use a non-bank money order, or do business with a pawn shop or rent-to-own business.

You're probably thinking: "Hey! I was underbanked at one point!" Of course you were. Many people who aren't starving, who aren't out on the streets—and who aren't being "overlooked" or "underserved" by banks—are, or at one point were, Underbanked.

According to the FDIC, only 10% of underbanked households use so-called alternative services because they don't have a bank account. Half, however, attribute their use to the convenience of AFS providers. And of the 24 million US households that the FDIC counts as Underbanked, 8.5 million—or 35%—make more than $50k a year.

Bottom line: We've got to stop using the term Underbanked. But the misuse and misconceptions surrounding the use of the term Underbanked isn't doing the industry any good. The confusion isn't limited to just the industry's leading publication, however.

A Knowledge@Wharton article titled A Question of Value: Bringing Banks to the Unbanked contains a number of statements that bear a closer degree of scrutiny.[47]

K@W: "One quarter of all Americans households are not maximizing their banks' services—or going to a bank at all—choosing instead to use such substitutes as check cashers, payday lenders and refund anticipation loans. [T]hese 34 million households are ostensibly on the radar of banks that could gain them as customers."

My take: First off, if "these 34 million households are on the radar of banks that could gain them as customers," then how could they be "not maximizing their banks' services" if they don't do business with banks? Second, why is it assumed that a customer who uses an alternative financial service provider is "not maximizing" their bank's services? Payday lending rates may be high, but direct deposit advances offered by banks and credit unions aren't exactly bargains. Assuming that one's bank could provide a service better than that offered by an alternative financial services providers is not a defensible assumption.

K@W: "Reaching out to these unbanked or underbanked consumers may become even more complicated due to an unintended consequence of the low interest rates set by the Federal Reserve in an effort to jumpstart the U.S. economy. As a result of the Fed's move, the story notes, banks are earning less on individual transactions, which means they will have to come up with new ways to make money. That might include raising fees for services, which in turn could lead to more consumers being priced out of doing business with traditional FIs."

My take: Banks have been raising fees for services for the past three years to recoup the revenues lost to the weak economy and regulatory changes. Many consumers have already been priced out of doing business with traditional banks. But...why is this assumed to be a negative? Who said that only a "traditional" financial institution could provide high-quality financial services to consumers?

This line of thinking seems to be rooted in some misguided belief that a checking account is some kind of God-given right, and that paying for the account (or at least paying more than some arbitrarily determined amount) is a violation of that right.

The EU seems to be moving in this direction. Given the financial troubles the EU is having, is this really a policy we want to emulate here in the US?

K@W: "Although the FDIC notes that the unbanked and underbanked sector in the U.S. tends to be composed mainly of "non-Asian minorities, lower-income households, younger households or unemployed households," this group is not a homogenous section of the population. Instead, they represent a range of races, incomes and ages "with different sets of needs and different challenges," notes Raul Vazquez, CEO of Progress Financial, a community-based financial services company targeting Latinos."

My take: Vazquez' comment is spot on. He blasts a common misconception that anyone who fits the label Unbanked or Underbanked is some kind of underprivileged consumer being taken advantage of by big evil financial institutions and alternative financial services providers.

Wrong assumption. There is a growing segment of the population called the Debanked—mainstream consumers who are highly educated, and either employed or employable (due to their current status as a college student)—who willingly, consciously, and rationally avoid doing business with a traditional FI.

K@W: "Many people do not like banks because they are tired of being charged fees that were explained in small print that no one reads," [Wharton Professor Keith] Weigelt points out. "They feel banks rip them off."

My take: Granted, disclosure statements could be simpler and easier to read. But one $5 fee doesn't put someone in dire straits. The people who pay out $1000+ per year in bank fees are doing so because of some so-called hidden fee. They do so because of their own behavior. They need help that banks aren't set up to do. An 2009 Aite Group analysis found that about one in five consumers with a bank account would be better off getting out of checking accounts and using prepaid debit cards to manage their finances. As fees have risen over the past three years, that percentage has to have grown.

The reality of the financial services industry is that for many consumers, using so-called alternative products from so-called alternative providers isn't a bad thing—it's a good thing.

And, in fact, that's exactly what Vazquez says:

"In order for the unbanked to begin relationships with traditional financial institutions, it might be necessary for them to first use community based organizations and other alternative products. "A bank is not necessarily built to meet the needs of these customers," he notes. "With the overhead [banks] carry and the fees they impose on accounts, [the cost] might be too high for an independent banking relationship."

My take: Vazquez is, again, spot on. But his comment hints at something I don't hear many people talking about: If the unbanked first use alternative providers before developing relationships with traditional FIs, then the unbanked aren't always unbanked. In other words, for many consumers, unbankedness is a transitory phase.

What this means is that, rather than creating regulatory hurdles and constraints that force traditional banks to serve the [temporarily] unbanked, public policy would be better served finding ways to fix the underlying factors causing the temporary unbankedness—which, in many cases, is temporary unemployment.

K@W: "Banks are eagerly trying to attract a chunk of this "underbanked" population, but are still looking for the best way to do it. Their desire to serve this customer base may not be so much out of goodwill, Weigelt notes, as the desire for higher profits."

My take: Banks have a desire for higher profits? Duh. But part of the statement above makes no sense, and is indicative of the confusion surrounding the terms unbanked and underbanked. By definition, the underbanked are already doing business with banks. So banks really aren't "looking for the best way" to attract them. They already have them. But, for whatever reasons, banks aren't providing all the products this segment needs. Maybe it's because they can't provide those products profitably. If that's the case, then banks really aren't looking to provide those services to this consumer segment.

There is no evidence that banks can't profitably provide those services.

Bottom line: Consumer advocate groups, industry pundits, and other uninformed observers need to understand this: So-called alternative products are no longer alternative. And that terms like unbanked and underbanked have outlived their usefulness.

It's time to kill the underbanked.

Why Some Consumers Are UnBanked

In a New York Times article titled *Over a Million Are Denied Bank Accounts for Past Errors,* the author writes:[48]

"Mistakes like a bounced check or a small overdraft have effectively blacklisted more than a million low-income Americans from the mainstream financial system for as long as seven years as a result of little-known private databases that are used by the nation's major banks. The problem is contributing to the growth of the roughly 10 million households in the United States that lack a banking account, a basic requirement of modern economic life. [T]he databases have ensnared millions of low-income Americans, according to interviews with financial counselors, consumer lawyers and more than two dozen low-income people."

I'm sure those 25 low-income people were representative of the overall low-income population in the US (sarcasm). There are a few problems with the Times' article:

1. **Databases don't "ensnare" anyone.** Poor choice of words on the Times' part, but what do you expect from a paper trying to emulate the National Enquirer? In any case, the databases track incidents, not demographics. According to a recent survey by Aite Group (sample size of 1,242, not "two dozen"), 51% of the consumers who were hit with an overdraft fee in 2012 earned more than $45k—i.e., not "low-income Americans." Looking at it from a different angle, among Americans earning less than $15k, 24% paid an overdraft fee in 2012. Among consumers earning between $70k and $100k, 25% paid an overdraft. These consumers are in the databases, by the way.

2. **The ranks of the unbanked have not "swelled."** The 2011 FDIC National Survey of Unbanked and Underbanked Households (which the NY Times cited) found that 8.2%

of US households were unbanked. As the FDIC put it, "the proportion of unbanked households increased slightly since the 2009 survey." Maybe the Times' spell checker inadvertently changed "slightly" to "swelled." Hey, it could happen. The unbanked ranks are not getting any bigger, let alone swelling.

3. **A bank account is not a "basic requirement of modern economic life."** When asked why they didn't have a bank account, the Unbanked don't list "denied by past errors" as the main reason. Here's what they do say (Table 11.1):

Table 11.1

How important are the following reasons for why you don't have a checking account?

	Very	Somewhat	Not
I don't want money withdrawn from my account without my permission	49%	17%	34%
I don't want to pay a bank's monthly fees	39%	25%	36%
I prefer to use a prepaid debit card	37%	24%	39%
Banks charge fees, like insufficient when a check bounces or a debit card is overdrawn	36%	26%	38%
I don't want to maintain minimum balance	30%	33%	37%
I have or had a credit issue or problems with a checking account in the past	29%	26%	45%
I need to have access to cash right away	22%	34%	44%
I prefer places where I can cash a check and pay my bills at the same time	16%	27%	57%
Banks' hours are not convenient for me	4%	16%	80%

Source: Aite Group/Chase Blueprint

Only 29% said that past credit issues or problems explained why they don't have a checking account, and in fact, nearly half (45%) said past problems were not a reason why they don't have an account.

On the other hand, 37% said that the reason they don't have an account is that they "prefer to use a prepaid debit card." In other words, they could get a checking account if they wanted to—but they don't want to. They've discovered that a checking account is not a "basic requirement of modern economic life."

Introducing the Debanked

There is a growing number of consumers in the United States who I call the Debanked:

Mainstream consumers who willingly opt out of the traditional banking system.

They're young, highly educated, employed (or employable)—and they're choosing to manage their financial lives without the help of a checking account, thank you very much.

They already use prepaid debit cards, and are highly satisfied with them (so please don't tell me about the weaknesses and downsides of prepaid debit cards, because what you and I think don't matter—these people are very satisfied with the cards).

And when they close out their checking accounts, between US$30 billion and US$40 billion in deposits are coming out. More importantly to banks, roughly US$1.7 billion in revenue (including overdraft fees, monthly fees, lending fees, and debit interchange) is coming off the banks' books. As a percentage of total banking industry revenues, US$1.7 billion might not be a lot, but there are reasons why this threat is important:

1. **The Debanked aren't "bad" customers.** Back during the Bank Transfer Day frenzy, I speculated that maybe Bank of America had done an analysis, and determined that the customers they would lose by imposing a fee for debit card use were unprofitable customers they could afford to lose. It's hard for me to see how the Debanked are bad customers. A larger-than-the-national-average percentage of them are college educated. Many are employed, and of those who aren't, it's because they're still students. They're heavy debit card users. And they bank and pay bills online, which the industry believes is a path to higher levels of customer retention and profitability.

2. **The Debanked might not be coming back.** Credit unions love to gloat about the number of people leaving big banks, but the reality is that not all are leaving for credit unions. Many are leaving the traditional banking system. Considering the relatively young age of the Debanked, and the desire on the part of pretty much every credit union out there to lower the average age of their member base, this doesn't bode well.

The Debanked may account for a small percentage of consumers today, but that number will grow rapidly over the next few years. According to Aite Group, roughly one in five checking account holders would consider giving up that product and switching entirely to a prepaid debit card.

The rise of the Debanked represents an important shift in society: For the first time in more than 60 years, young people entering adulthood are not automatically opening up a checking account.

When my generation—Baby Boomers—went into the working world, those of us whose brains weren't fried from LSD and marijuana opened up a checking account. Actually, many of us opened a second account, because we had one in college, from a bank that we vowed to never do business with again.

When Gen Xers went into the working world, (among those whose septums weren't deviated from too much cocaine) they opened up a checking account. Didn't think twice about it.

But today, it's different. It's not an automatic thing for Gen Yers to open up a checking account (the fact that many struggle to enter the working world is part of it, but not all of it). They don't write checks (many actually don't know how). They want alternatives.

Alternatives like NeoChecking accounts.

The Rise of NeoChecking and Neo Banks

Green Dot, a leading provider of prepaid debit cards, recently launched a new type of FDIC-insured DDA (demand deposit account) that is opened, and fully serviced, on a mobile app running a smartphone.

The app includes a savings vault that allows customers to move money into a savings account without gaining access through the debit card, bill pay which includes P2P payment capability, and an ability to easily load funds through direct deposit, RDC or cash at Walmart locations. The Fortune Teller budgeting tool provides point-of-sale advice on the impact of a purchase on the customer's budget.

The account will charge $2.50 per ATM transaction for out of network ATMs, a 3% foreign transaction fee with the debit card, and $9 to customize the card design. Overall, Green Dot expects four revenue streams from the product: 1) Debit interchange income (the firm has less than $10b in assets, so no rate cap); 2) Service fees; 3) Float on deposits; and 4) A voluntary monthly fee of up to $9 (no, I'm not joking).

GoBank targets consumers with less than US$100k income, does not plan to add a credit product, and does not think the new offering will cannibalize its GPR (general purpose, reloadable) prepaid debit card business.

My take: GoBank represents a new type of product in the market, which, for lack of a better name, I call a NeoChecking account, and a new type of startup bank, or NeoBank.

Other than prepaid card accounts, there are few real alternatives to checking accounts available today for the Debanked (and consumers that would like to de-bank). That's what's changing with accounts from companies like GoBank and Moven. They're not just alternatives to banks—they're creating alternatives to checking accounts.

When I mentioned to Moven founder Brett King that I was calling this new type of account a NeoChecking account, he said:

> "Don't use 'check' because one of the key behaviors of the new account type is the anti-check behavior."

King's premise that a key driver behind consumers' use of prepaid debit cards is that they don't need checks, but need a card is spot on.

But I don't have a better name for this new account. "Spend account" or "transaction account" doesn't seem new or sexy enough. So I'm going with NeoChecking Account. If nothing else, Keanu Reeves will like it.

Regarding the emergence of NeoChecking accounts:

1. **Mobile-centricity is a no-brainer.** GoBank's and Moven's emphasis on being mobile-first, branchless, and (possibly) cardless is not a big deal. Every bank has mobile banking or will. Well-established banks like USAA could probably wipe the floor with GoBank and Moven when it comes to mobile capabilities. I've seen critical reviews of the mobile apps from some large banks. That's fixable. It's no big news that the startups focus on mobile. They're not going to build a branch network, and they're going to focus on the

group of consumers who are not entrenched in their financial relationships, and who represent the disproportionate share of demand for financial accounts—Gen Yers. This segment relies so heavily on their mobile device for everything, they're sleeping with it, and taking it places I'd rather not talk about.

2. **Consumer interest in NeoBanks isn't about the desire for a new kind of bank.** Startups and non-mainstream banks (e.g., Ally) love to tout how they're a "new" kind of bank, and love to cite the low consumer trust numbers that research has reported over the past few years. Who cares? The top 50 banks grew deposits by 8.5% for the 12 months ending June 2012 while credit unions' share balances increased 6.0% (from October 2011 through September 2012). Big banks like Wells Fargo, JPMorganChase, US Bank, and PNC each had deposit growth about double the credit union total. People want a new type of bank? Nonsense. They want a new type of account.

NeoChecking Accounts: Not For NeoBanks Only

The traditional checking account generates a lot of revenue for banks, but mostly through non-value added (from the customer's perspective) fees like overdraft fees, ATM fees, inactivity fees, and whatever other penalties banks (and credit unions) dream up.

The value proposition of a NeoChecking account is that it provides value to the customer. The theory is that consumers will be more accepting of paying a fee to use the product (I am not going to go as far as saying that consumers will "want" to pay a fee).

There are a couple of NeoChecking alternatives available to banks and credit unions today, and one that I'd like to see:

1) **Kasasa.** The notion of a checking account created by a third-party non-bank entity, but offered by a bank or credit union, is foreign to traditional bankers. But that's exactly what Kasasa is. And it's proving to be highly successful for the community banks and credit unions that offer it—even though some of them are in similar geographies. It's not just the brand power of Kasasa (the product) that helps bring in new customers to the banks that offer it. It's the underlying marketing competencies that BancVue, the company that developed Kasasa, brings to the table—marketing competencies that many community banks and credit unions could never develop on their own.

   Why is Kasasa an example of NeoChecking? As a product branded separately from the financial institution that provides it, a bank or credit union that offers Kasasa is, in effect, telling its customers, "we'll offer the right products for you regardless of who offers it." The value proposition of a NeoBank's NeoChecking accounts is "adding value to customers" and "helping them make the right decision." A community bank or credit union offering Kasasa is projecting that value, as well. Not to mention, leveraging the brand awareness, pull, and profitability that Kasasa provides.

2) **BaZing.** This product, from StrategyCorps, promises to deliver about $75 in fee income per year from 40% of existing checking accounts and 30% of new accounts opened (and higher percentages if the bank doesn't charge for the account). Why would a consumer pay for this type of account? To get benefits not traditionally associated with a checking account like health and prescription savings, cell phone protection, and ID theft aid.

3) **The Merchant-Funded Account.** This one doesn't exist yet (If I'm wrong, somebody will let me know). This type

of account would be pitched as a "free" checking account if the customer accepts some number (or dollar amount) of merchant-funded offers on a monthly basis. In effect, the customer buys his or her way out of a monthly fee (not unlike what a lot of banks do today with account balances and/or opening additional products). Response rates on offers would go up astronomically because customers would have to redeem, increasing the incentive for retailers and merchants to participate.

The features—or value propositions—of these NeoChecking accounts aren't foreign to existing banks and accounts. The problem is in the execution. Banks throw in these features on top of existing account functionality and—more importantly—on top of the existing price structure.

By giving away value-added features in the context of an account that continues to hit the customer with penalties and non-value added fees (sorry, but consumers simply don't see $35 of value in an overdraft situation), the perceived value of the feature is diminished.

One point we need to discuss here: The value of merchant-funded offers (MFOs).

I remain a strong believer that consumers' purchase data can be effectively used in marketing efforts.

But not from the perspective of convincing consumers that they're getting more relevant offers (and certainly not that they're getting more relevant offers). The benefit of MFOs is to the retailer/merchant. In terms of reaching consumers who demonstrate certain purchase behaviors in a particular category.

Today, retailers and merchants have NO clue what any individual consumer spends on products in their category, and usually doesn't even know how much that consumers spends with them.

The value of the MFO concept is in helping marketers improve their customer acquisition efforts. Today, they spend billions of dollars in poorly targeted mass media channels. The promised benefit of marketing MFOs through banks is increased efficiency of spend, and measurability (which Twitter really sucks at, by the way).

Consumers do not care about MFOs. It is not a selling point to a checking account. The promise that they will save money on the purchases "they already make" by signing up with MFOs doesn't fool anyone. Consumers believe that they get the same coupons and deals from any number of sources.

By the way: If the MFOs I'm seeing from my bank are based on my actual purchases, then someone has stolen my identity and is using my debit card at hair and nail salons all over Massachusetts.

Are NeoBanks Disruptive?

If I had a nickel for every time the word "disruption" was mentioned in a blog post, article, or conference, I'd be richer than Warren Buffett. If I had a nickel for every time the word was appropriately used, I wouldn't be able to afford one share of his company's stock.

Wikipedia's definition of "disruptive innovation" is:[49]

> "An innovation that helps create a new market and value network, and eventually goes on to disrupt an existing market and value network (over a few years or decades), displacing an earlier technology. The term is used in business and technology literature to describe innovations that improve a product or service in ways that the market does not expect, typically first by designing for a different set of consumers in a new market and later by lowering prices in the existing market."

There is no shortage of startups in banking—at the top of the list being the NeoBanks—that claim to be disruptive. Most (if not all) of them, however, aren't disruptive in the least. What they really do is fill niches in the current market by serving unmet needs. According to Wikipedia:[50]

> "The automobile was a revolutionary technological innovation, but it was not a disruptive innovation, because early automobiles were expensive luxury items that did not disrupt the market for horse-drawn vehicles. The market for transportation essentially remained intact until the debut of the lower priced Ford Model T in 1908. The mass-produced automobile was a disruptive innovation, because it changed the transportation market. The automobile, by itself, was not."

Sounds like today's banking industry, no?

Startups are finding cracks in the market by serving people who don't want to pay checking account fees, or who don't like banks and want to find an alternative. But these startups aren't disruptive. They're not creating new markets—they're simply meeting the unmet needs of the existing one.

And they won't be anywhere close to being disruptive until they develop some kind of technology that is adopted by other providers of financial services. In other words, just gaining market share in an existing market doesn't qualify a firm as disruptive. Ford was the first to mass-produce cars, but mass-produced cars only became a disruptive technology when other manufacturers adopted it as well.

The Fat Lady Ain't Singing

Claims of disruption and disintermediation are heard on a nearly daily basis in the press and blogosphere. One of the more popular analogies that is raised, from time to time, is the music industry.

An American Banker article titled *Time to Face the Music On Disintermediation* stated:[51]

"In spite of all the regulation that helps prop up legacy business models and protect established companies, much of banking is ripe for digital disintermediation-and it's starting to happen already. Fundamentally, banks connect those with money to those who need it. By limiting access to the systems that handle the transactions, banks have been able to charge big fees. But the walls are breaking down now, just like they did in the music business."

My take: The banking and music industries aren't analogous. In response to the article, banker David Gerbino tweeted "I disagree. Banks/CUs are embracing change. The music industry tried to stop it." Gerbino is right, but there are other reasons why the viewpoints in the article are off-base, and why the music industry suffered what it did:

1. **The product form changed...** Although the music industry saw plenty of change in product form from 1950 to 2000 (from vinyl to cassettes to CDs), one thing was constant: The product was a physical product. It wasn't until music became a predominantly virtual product that the industry began to suffer.

2. **...which caused the cost of production to plunge...** In and of itself, the digitization of music doesn't explain that industry's woes. Another contributor is that, as a result of this digitization, the cost of producing the product dropped. Virtually any musician could produce a high-quality mp3 file.

3. **...and caused the cost of distribution to plummet...** In addition to making it easy to produce the product, musicians could easily do an end-run around the traditional distribution channels and go direct to their fans.

4. **...which exacerbated intellectual property rights...** The fly in the ointment—illegal file sharing—became more like a Mothra in the ointment thanks to Napster and subsequently other sites. This created a need for new approaches and new firms with the capability of protecting and enforcing these rights.

5. **...and resulted in new business models.** iTunes and other companies emerged to fill the need. Today, people subscribe to music online. And it's even getting worse for traditional players in the industry. Recently, I watched Bob Weir's band Ratdog broadcast a live concert from his new TRI Studios in Marin County. It was free, and attracted about 100,000 viewers. They could have easily charged $5 and with even just 20,000 views grossed $100,000. The variable costs of touring from city to city can be avoided.

Now let's look at the banking industry:

1. **The product form hasn't changed.** I find it interesting that the author of the article says that banks "fundamentally connect those with money to those who need it." That's one part of the business. But payments—think of this as the "transfer of funds"—make up a pretty big portion of what a bank does, no? When you write a check, or use your debit card against your bank account, you are fundamentally triggering a transfer of funds from your account to someone else's. It's certainly true that access mechanisms—how we check our balances, transfer funds between our own accounts, etc.—has changed, and become more electronic. But the underlying form of the product has been electronic for some time now.

2. **The need for security drives up costs.** As far as I know, no one has tried to steal the music off my hard drive (it's mostly Grateful Dead concerts). But protecting the funds in my account is a pretty big deal. And as most

banks know, it requires a lot of investment to ensure that accounts are protected from fraudulent activity. So-called disintermediators to the banking industry often seriously underestimate the cost of doing this.

3. **Risk management is a requirement.** Security and fraud are one thing, risk management is another. When a bank makes a payment it often assumes the risk of non-payment (something Dick Durbin can't seem to understand). Any potential newcomer can design a fancy front-end website to disintermediate the banks. But that doesn't alleviate the need for risk management.

4. **Regulations create barriers to entry.** While the bank haters love to point to regulations as something that keeps the barriers to entry erected, most bankers know that there are scores of regulations that drive up costs and eat into profitability (the largest 100 banks in the US spend US$1 billion on compliance each year, according to my estimates). Potential disintermediators looking to get into the industry must adapt to the regulatory environment.

In fact, one of the author's examples shows how banks' role is strengthened, not disintermediated: Square. Today, many micro-merchants are forced to accept cash or checks from their customers because they haven't been able to accept credit cards. By outfitting these merchants with card readers, more payments can actually flow through the banks that issue credit cards.

Another of the author's examples—Simple—does create a new interface to banks, but doesn't eliminate banks from the equation.

Bottom line: Because of the complexity of moving money— including technological complexity, security concerns, risk management needs, and regulatory compliance—banks won't be disintermediated a la the music industry. The fat lady may be singing to the big music companies, but she ain't singing to the banks. Not yet, at least.

All of this is not to say that we won't see new entrants into the industry. Just not until new business models emerge and take hold.

HUMOR BREAK
DEAR DICK DURBIN

The US government, in its infinite wisdom, decided to apply an approach called "reasonable debit fee transaction" when determining how to set the debit card interchange rate back in 2010.

The banking industry, understandably, was opposed to this approach. I saw it differently. Here's my open letter to Senator Dick Durbin, the author of the legislation:

Dear Dick

A lot of folks in the financial services industry are ticked off about your "reasonable debit fee" legislation.

Don't listen to them. They're 180 degrees wrong. Not only should we not back off from the reasonable fee approach, we need to extend it to other areas outside of financial services. Here's where you need to start:

iPads. Apple wants to charge $700-800 for these things? WTF. According to BusinessWeek, the components for an iPad costs like $260. "Reasonable fees" suggests that this is capitalist pig price gouging on the part of Apple. You should give the FTC the authority to set a "reasonable" price for iPads.

Cars. Best as I can tell, Ferrari doesn't use some special and rare magno-titanium to produce their cars. Doesn't cost that much more to make than it takes to manufacture my Yugo. "Reasonable fees" says these things should cost $25k—not $250k.

Houses. There is no reason why that pile of wood and concrete you live in should cost $1 million. The wood probably cost $150. Labor to build it: $1000. The land it was built on: Already there. But I guess it did cost $100 to have someone level it. "Reasonable fees" says you should get ~$10k for that house.

And when a representative from MasterCard writes...

"Debit interchange on prepaid cards effectively allows the government to save taxpayers money by putting disbursements from unemployment insurance and child support to social security and disability payments onto prepaid cards instead of checks with no or very low cost"

...you should feel free to consider this to be the ranting of some lunatic. I mean, after all, with the changes you've proposed and what the administration is doing for the economy, unemployment should be eradicated completely in a few months, so who's going to need these cards anyway? Right? Really now, the nerve of someone proposing to keep the cost of government down. Sheesh.

So stand strong Mr. D, and don't let these bankers rattle you. And let's get working to extend reasonable fees to other industries and areas of the economy. Because that would only be "fair," right?

All the best,

Ron

Part IV
The New Technologies

Chapter Twelve
The Unfulfilled Promise
of PFM

Financial services executives sure are optimistic about the impact that online personal financial management (PFM) could have on customers. The following quotes were pulled from CU Times:

> "We wanted to bring a product to market that offered our members a real and complete solution to managing their personal finances."—Credit union COO, referring to PFM

> "The purpose of [PFM] is to help build awareness of the credit union's ability to help individuals plan for short- and long-term financial goals, as well as track income and expenses and promote financial literacy."—Credit union

> "Gaining an understanding of one's financial picture will empower our members to make prudent financial decisions."—Credit union CEO

Are these quotes realistic? On one hand, there is research to support the contentions. Aite Group's research into the impact of PFM on consumers' financial lives shows that PFM:[52]

- Impacts users' financial lives. An overwhelming percentage of users say PFM has given them control over their financial lives, many are saying that they're saving more money as a result of using PFM (and a majority of Gen Y users, I might add), and a good chunk are paying less in overdraft fees, late fees, and interest.

- Impacts users' relationship with their banks. Compared to consumers who don't use PFM, a higher percentage of consumers who use PFM tools credit PFM with making them more likely to stay with their bank and to consider their bank for their future product needs.

So what's the problem? Why is there an "unfulfilled promise"?

The PFM Benefits Pyramid

As implemented by most banks today, PFM is little more than tools for budgeting, expense categorization, and cash flow analysis. As a result, PFM falls short of delivering the value and impact hoped for, or expected, by the execs quoted at the beginning of the chapter.

Which isn't to say that PFM doesn't have any impact. It does. Broadly speaking, the impact of PFM falls into three categories: 1) Oversight (knowing where someone's money is and where it goes); 2) Insight (the ability to better control and manage their financial accounts); and 3) Foresight (the ability to make better financial decisions).[53]

The problem, or unfulfilled promise, is that relatively few PFM users reap all the potential benefits. Among the 20% of consumers that use online PFM tools, about half are reaping "oversight" benefits. Only 35% of PFM users—7% of the total population—use PFM to better control and manage their financial lives. And 18% of PFM users—less than 4% of the overall consumer population—are making better financial decisions, and saving on fees, rates, and interest payments, as a result of using online PFM tools (Figure 12.1).

Figure 12.1

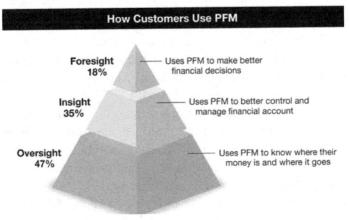

Source: Aite Group

Bottom line: Few PFM users have reached the pinnacle (or the middle level) of this pyramid. Budgeting and expense categorization, with pretty charts and graphs, simply doesn't have that much of an impact on consumers' financial lives.

Redefining PFM

In a blog post titled *Will Mobile Finally Make PFM Popular?*, Jim Bruene, publisher of NetBanker wrote:[54]

> "There are currently five specialty PFMs [BillGuard, Lemon, Manilla, Credit Karma, and Mint] in the 13 most-downloaded free finance apps. Mobile is, and will be, a huge driver for specialty PFM apps. App stores help consumers find the services, and mobile makes them less daunting to use. But it's not just the mobile platform driving usage at the four challengers [to Mint], it's the way they have posi-

tioned themselves with tangible consumer benefits (e.g., save money by spotting fraud charges) rather than the nebulous (e.g., "manage your spending for a better life"). Only Mint is positioned as a pure PFM. The challengers are all backing into PFM from various niches."

The last two sentences in the quote intrigue me. What is a "pure" PFM? Why does Bruene think that the firms listed in the post are "challengers" to Mint? And why does he think those challengers are "backing into" PFM?

The core of the issue is simple: There is no clear definition about what PFM is (and isn't). There is no common understanding—among bankers or consumers—about what PFM is. If you showed consumers a list of companies that included Mint, BillGuard, Lemon, Credit Karma, and Manilla, and asked: "Which of these companies offers a "pure" PFM?" you would get blank stares from 98% of them.

Even among bankers, the term PFM is too loosely used. When Bruene refers to Mint as a "pure" PFM, he mean a PFM platform that offers budgeting, expense categorization, and charting, forecasting, analysis tools. Geezeo and Money Desktop, which offer their technologies through banks, rather than direct to consumers like Mint, would be considered "pure" PFM tools, as well. Within the banking community, the term PFM encompasses budgeting, expense categorization, charting, forecasting, and analysis tools.

But few consumers have shown interest in these capabilities. Instead, they want to know their credit score, how it's changing, and what to do about it (Credit Karma), or they want to track or prevent grey charges on their debit and credit cards (BillGuard).

These capabilities are "personal financial management" capabilities. They're not "backing in" to PFM. They are PFM. And they're not challenging Mint (or other "pure" PFM platforms)—they're providing additional capabilities not found in Mint.

I'm a big fan of what the "pure" PFM players are doing. But bankers need to redefine their concept of PFM, and expand the definition to include a wider range of "PFM" capabilities.

What they'll realize is that their "pure" PFM deployments fall well short of providing the range of capabilities that consumers want and need. And they'll realize that their "pure" PFM deployments need to become more of a platform that integrates the "challengers" into the platform.

It won't be the Apps Stores that help consumers find the "specialty" financial apps out there. It will be the banks and credit unions. The banks will vet the apps, recommend to their customers which ones are good, safe, and can be integrated. Consumers will pay for these apps, and FIs will get a cut of the revenue for helping the developers reach a wider base of users.

To get back to the core question of the NetBanker post—will mobile finally make PFM popular?—the answer is: "It depends on how you define PFM."

If the industry continues to have a narrow definition of PFM (i.e., budgeting, expense categorization), then the answer is NO.

On the other hand, if it defines PFM more broadly, then the answer is YES.

But a lot of bankers still won't grasp the strategic importance of this. It represents a shift in the underlying value of banking.

The old value was money movement. Banks are good at moving money. You parked your paycheck in the bank, then wrote checks (and more recently swiped your debit card) to pay for things, and the bank took care of moving the money.

The new value is money management. Despite the flagging economy and all the talk of the "1%", the numbers don't lie: Compared to even 20 years ago, Americans' earning and spending power is as strong as ever.

According to data published by the Federal Reserve Bank of St. Louis, in the United States between 1992 and 2012, quarterly real retail and food services sales—adjusted for inflation—grew by nearly 50% to nearly US$180 billion, returning to pre-recession (i.e., prior to 2008) levels.[55]

Think FPM, Not PFM

Many consumers don't want, or don't need, help allocating and investing assets, managing budgets, or categorizing expenses. But many do want help making smart(er) choices about how they spend and manage their money.

I'm not one to shy away from naming things, so I've got a name and an acronym for what is needed: Financial Performance Management (FPM).

Consumers need tools like the bill analysis tools that Truaxis provides, the card and mortgage analysis tools that Credit Sesame has developed, the saving incentives apps that Bobber Interactive has designed, and the spend management capabilities that Banno has developed.

But consumers need these things to work together with their existing accounts, and existing online and mobile banking platforms. Independent, one-off tools and sites will never gain enough traction to garner a significant mass of consumers.

If banks really want to provide their customers and members with a "complete solution to managing their personal finances," they'll have to go well beyond slapping up some PFM (i.e., budgeting and expense categorization) tools on their web sites.

It's going to require a concerted and strategic effort on banks' part to bring these capabilities together into a coherent offering.

Adding PFM as a feature to checking accounts is a dead end.

FPM needs to become the product. It's what people will pay for. It's what delivers the value.

Humor Break
What Would You Name Your
New Bank?

With all the talk about Google, Apple, and Amazon becoming (or starting) banks, it got me thinking: If other industries started banks, what would they call them?

Fast food: This bank would be the model of operational efficiency—it would get people in and out the door efficiently. Product quality wouldn't be that good (of course, that would be no different from today's banks). And it would be great at trying to up-sell you something at the point of transaction (of course, that would be no different from today's banks). Bank names: Savings King, In-and-out Bank, and Whatabank.

Internet: Every product offered by this bank would be in perpetual beta release (Checking Account ver 1.3.4b). Customer service would be non-existent (of course, that would be no different from today's banks), and the bank's Web site would be very colorful, with lots of cool graphics. Bank names: Knab, Yemon.

Automotive: This bank would publish a list of exorbitant fees that it would discount based on each customer's ability to negotiate (of course, that would be no different from today's banks). Bank names: LeBank, Bankeville.

Chapter Thirteen
The Social Media Mirage

Dictionary.com's definition of mirage is "something illusory, without substance or reality."

That's a pretty good description of the view that many social media gurus have regarding the potential impact of social media on customer relationships and company profitability. Especially in banking.

I don't dispute that social media holds the potential to help firms build stronger relationships with its customers—and even contribute to the trust that consumers have with the firms (brands) they do business with. But many people are overstating the contribution to trust that social media will make, because they have no understanding of what goes in to building trust, and if there are two steps, twenty steps, or no steps.

There's an illness called Silverbulletitis that plagues many marketers:

A condition in which the sufferer expects easy answers and solutions to difficult problems.

This condition has been prevalent in banking for a long time. Online banking, online bill pay, eBills, and PFM have all taken a turn as the silver bullet, each touted as the panacea for repairing poor customer relationships.

Social media is now taking its turn on that list.

A report from financial services communications firm Cicero made this claim:[56]

"Social media offers the financial services sector an opportunity to resuscitate its relationship with the public after the financial crisis."

My first reaction: Oh really? Prove it! The study's attempt to prove it isn't very convincing:

- "25% of respondents felt that social media offers a new way to communicate to tomorrow's consumers." This means, of course, that the vast majority of respondents—75%—don't feel that social media offers a new way to communicate to tomorrow's consumers. In highlighting this finding, is the communications firm implying that these 75% somehow "don't get it" when it comes to social media? Maybe the 75% have tried social media and have found that it doesn't offer a new way to communicate.

- "30% of those surveyed see social media as the future of communications." Again, an interesting choice of which number to highlight, since this finding implies that the majority—70%—don't see social media as the future of communications. After the study highlights the fact that Facebook reached 50 million users in less than four years, it goes on to show that just 22% of survey respondents believe that "consumers respond to social media." Are the respondents clueless or do they know this from experience?

- "One quarter of respondents are daunted by the volume of traffic on social media and how to monitor and manage it." By now, you should be getting pretty good about doing the math, and have already figured out that 75%—or what we could call the "vast majority"—don't find social media volume daunting, or find the monitoring and managing of it to be daunting.

The question, or issue, here is this: Are financial services executives somehow missing the boat on something that social media proponents are seeing and advocating for?

If you read the mainstream media, it might be easy to come to the conclusion that financial services executives are evil morons, clueless about how to develop customer relationships. Given the decline in the traditional mainstream media, this is the pot calling the kettle black.

There is a popular sentiment that the financial services industry is a "laggard" when it comes to social media, or is "struggling" with it.

But the evidence doesn't support that. What the evidence supports is that financial services firms are doing plenty of things with social media—and that they aren't seeing huge, transformational results.

This conclusion isn't based on just the viewpoints of bankers.

A 2011 Aite Group report based on a survey of more than 400 financial advisors, found that the percentage of advisors that have reaped benefits from social media declined from 2009, as did the percentage that said that social media is a strong contributor to a range of key business objectives.[57]

One of the key messages I tried to get across to wealth management firms who were looking to help the advisors they support use social media was this: Social media does not make you a good marketer. Good marketers figure out how to effectively use social media.

Bottom line: While financial services executives have shown signs of silverbulletitis in the past, there is growing evidence that many are not drinking the kool-aid this time around, as it concerns social media. Social media proponents need to prove claims that social media can have a dramatic impact on customer relationships with theories and explanations for why social media is superior to communicating through firms' web sites, call centers, and branches.

The Social Media Measurement Malaise

According to a Social Media Today article titled *Can Financial Services and Social Media Co-Exist and Succeed?*:[58]

> "Securian Financial Group, a Minnesota-based insurance and financial services company forged ahead with a social media pilot program that generated some compelling results."

According to the company's communications manager, "We picked a topic, 'Long-term goals need a long-term partner,' that was representative of our brand and comfortable for our compliance department. We hired a small crew, walked to a local park and conducted spontaneous interviews."

The interviews became a series of four videos which were posted on Securian's YouTube channel, and promoted on the corporate Facebook and Twitter pages.

According to the article, the campaign strove to: 1) Increase Facebook "Likes" by 25%; 2) Increase Twitter followers by 15%; 3) Build brand recognition for Securian; and 4) Promote Securian's commitment to helping people reach their long-term financial goals.

The company's Facebook page likes rose 27% to 571 and Twitter followers increased by 19% to 191.

My take: Compelling results, my foot.

The insurer got roughly 120 new likes (if they started with 451 likes, an increase of 120 = 27%), while Twitter followers grew from about 160 to 191 (a 19% increase). I'm not calling anyone a liar (or maybe I am), but it seems pretty fishy to me that the actual results were 27% and 19%, respectively. How did Securian determine that likes should increase by 25%, and followers by 15%?

I don't think that Securian had any idea how many likes and followers they would get. If you haven't done this kind of thing before, how could you possibly predict the results? Do other insurance companies publish the results of their social media experiments to provide a guide for other insurers? Of course not.

I can imagine the conversation that went on in this company:

Social media ninja: "Hey, I have a great idea. Let's interview people about insurance, and put the videos on YouTube. I think we can get 100 Facebook page likes and 25 new Twitter followers if we do this. We have $2,500 in our social media marketing budget. We can use it to hire a camera crew."

CMO: "Great idea. Syncapse says that the value of a Facebook like is $136, and Clickz published something saying that the value of a Twitter follower is $2.50. So if we get 100 new likes and 25 new followers, and invest $2,500, the ROI will be about 447%."

I think we both know that this wasn't the way it happened—in fact, the Communications Manager at Securian is quoted as saying that they went into this as an experiment.

I'm not knocking Securian here. They have $850 billion of insurance in force, $35 billion of assets under management, and 10 million clients. They can afford to throw $2,500 into creating some YouTube videos without any expectation (or calculation) of a payoff.

But I'm willing to bet that Securian doesn't know if its efforts have paid off already or not. After all, exactly who are these people that liked the Facebook page? Are they existing customers? Prospects? I bet that Securian doesn't know.

I do hope, however, for Securian's sake, that the Likes are from one of the two categories above, and not from employees.

A few years back, Washington Mutual (WaMu) beat its chest in press releases that, within 48 hours of launching a Facebook page, it had a couple of hundred fans.

At the time, I snooped around and found that at least three-quarters of those fans were affiliated in one way or another with the ad agency that did the design work for the bank's Facebook page. So not only were these fans not worth $136 to the bank, but in essence, as a vendor to the bank, they cost the bank money.

(Which reminds me: If the ROI of social media is not going out of business, and WaMu invested in social media and still went out of business, then… oh, never mind).

What we have here is Social Media Today looking for an example of a financial services firm doing something with social media, and spinning the results to make them look good. So they can say "See? Social media really works. Honest it does."

But it doesn't pass the test of scrutiny. Thirty-one new Twitter followers is not a "compelling" result. I get that many new followers each week, not by shooting videos, but by shooting my mouth off.

The problem here isn't simply the use of vanity metrics. It's the lack of a marketing measurement infrastructure.

If Securian's social media efforts are truly driving brand awareness and affinity, how is it measuring that—regardless of the channel used to drive those objectives?

And how does brand awareness and affinity drive number of qualified leads? After all, insurance people like to say that "insurance isn't bought, it's sold," so if you're not generating leads, you're wasting your time.

If Securian is measuring those things, great.

But the problem here isn't with what Securian is or isn't doing—it's with measuring social media in a vacuum.

Social Media Metrics Are a Waste of Time

According to a Harvard Business Review (HBR) blog post titled *Why Your Social Media Metrics Are A Waste Of Time*:[59]

"Many companies use the wrong metrics to measure their performance, especially when it comes to social media. If you think page views, unique visitors, registered members, conversion rates, email-newsletter open rates, number of Twitter followers, or Facebook likes are important by themselves, you probably have no idea what you're doing."

"Here are four of the most important metrics you can follow—notice how little they have to do with popular social-media metrics: 1) Relevant revenue; 2) Sales volume; 3) Customer retention; and 4) Relevant growth. These metrics are valuable because they measure success at your core business. To measure the value of your social-media activities, you have to look at the results the company is getting overall and track how social media was involved in moving the needle. That's where you'll find the only relevant social-media metrics."

The key sentence: "To measure the value of your social-media activities, you have to look at the results the company is getting overall and track how social media was involved in moving the needle."

Technically, correct. Practically, useless.

Of the many challenges facing marketers, attribution of results to investments is one of the stickiest. Many marketers design tests to see which offer tests better, or which web page design delivers the highest conversion rate. But tying overall revenue, retention, and growth to social media metrics—in the absence of control groups or other structured testing techniques—is, for the most part, impossible.

Not that that won't stop marketers from using correlative measures. But it doesn't prove causation. Unless you only touch a customer through social media, you can't claim that social media was the cause of any change in the relationship.

In the absence of solid prescription and advice on how to tie social media efforts to bottom-line results, blog posts like the one from HBR are the real waste of time.

It's not that metrics like page views, unique visitors, or number of followers are the "wrong metrics" to use. It's that marketers must: 1) evaluate metrics in the context of a "metrics funnel," and 2) consider the cost of measuring metrics.

Few (if any) marketers have done the hard work to understand if and how metrics like page views, visitors, or followers impact the bottom-line metrics the author of the article wants us to measure.

Marketers need to think of marketing metrics as following a funnel, from upstream metrics like page views and follows to downstream metrics like sales, revenue, and retention.

What about midstream metrics? This is where the concept of customer engagement comes in. What are the things that good customers do—that demonstrate engagement—after they've viewed a page, liked your Facebook page, or visited your site that lead to increased sales and/or retention?

The problem isn't that upstream metrics are the "wrong" metrics to measure—it's that they're an insufficient set of metrics to use to measure performance.

But that's just the first of the two issues causing problems. The second is that it costs money to develop and track a metric.

Some metrics—like page views, followers, likes, etc.—are easy and cheap to measure. But developing those midstream metrics, and determining the linkage between upstream, midstream, and downstream metrics are harder to define and measure. And it takes an investment on the part of Marketing to develop and track them.

What's the ROI on that investment?

There is none. Spending money to develop and track and metric in and of itself will have no impact on the bottom line. You might be able to use that metric to make better decisions that ultimately lead to improved sales or reduced costs, but simply defining and calculating a metric doesn't produce that result.

So what happens is that Marketing doesn't invest in a measurement infrastructure. It defaults to tracking the easy-and-cheap-to-measure metrics. The ones the author of the HBR article thinks are the "wrong" metrics.

To Track or Not To Track: That Is The Question

The most important question to address isn't "what social media metrics should we be tracking?" but "should we even spend time and money developing social media metrics to track?"

Here's why: Assume that a company's marketing budget is $100 million, and that 50% of it is spent on TV advertising, 20% on print advertising, 20% on direct mail, 5% on online advertising, 4% on events, and 1% on social media.

Of the six approaches that marketing invests in, which of the six would you want to have the most accurate marketing ROI metrics?

My top three would be TV, print, and direct mail. Cuz that's where 90% of the marketing dollars go.

If the CMO of my fictional company doesn't have the "right" social media metrics in place, so what? Does it really matter that much?

Now, I can already hear the gurus claiming that social media has a disproportionate impact on customer relationships.

Maybe that's true. But that just means the CMO of my fictional company needs to know if s/he should reallocate investments between the six categories in some other way than it's being allocated today.

It doesn't mean investing more in a social media measure-ment infrastructure. It means investing more to develop a marketing measurement infrastructure. And that puts many Marketing departments in a chicken-and-egg situation: Can't prove the ROI of their investments, but can't afford to invest in a measurement infrastructure to improve the measurement of marketing ROI.

On the Other Hand: Why You Should Measure Social Media ROI

IBM discovered something it called the Perception Gap (Figure 13.1):60

Figure 13.1

Source: IBM Institute of Business Value

There are a number of things to take away from this chart, but the two most important are:

1. **Businesses think consumers connect with them on social sites for lots of reasons.** Who knows how many things IBM prompted for in their study, but at least 60% of business respondents cited 12 reasons why consumers connect with them. On the other hand, only one reason garnered

at least 60% of consumers' responses for why they connect to businesses.

2. **Few consumers connect with businesses to "feel connected" or "be part of a community."** Just one in three consumers connect with businesses to feel connected, and barely one in five do so to be part of a community. Nearly two-thirds of businesses, however, think consumers follow them to feel connected, and roughly six in 10 think consumers do so to be part of a community.

IBM calls this a perception gap. I call it delusion.

This has important implications for how firms should design their social media sites, and just as importantly, which metrics they use to measure the success of their social media efforts.

In a study titled *Why Do People Use Social Media? Empirical Findings and a New Theoretical Framework for Social Media Goal Pursuit*, Donna Hoffman and Thomas Novak from the University of California, Riverside identified seven "goal factors" including:

1. Learn—find information about interests, interact with groups that share my interests, etc.

2. Socialize—socialize with friends/family, reconnect with people I've lost touch with, etc.

3. Network—network for business/professional purposes, promote myself or business, etc.

4. Update status—tell people what I'm doing, find out what others are doing, etc.

5. Shop—find information about products, find good deals, etc.

6. New people—meet new people, socialize with anonymous people, etc.

7. Media fun—find and share music/videos, etc.

What IBM's study shows—as it applies to consumer-to-business social media behavior—is that consumers are not looking to satisfy all of the needs identified in the Hoffman/Novak study. Understanding consumers' goals—and the relative importance of each goal—should drive firms' social media site design.

Regarding social media metrics, some social media gurus advise firms to not measure the ROI of their social media efforts and to look at alternative metrics. The author of *5 Ways to Measure Social Media Success on the Business2Community site asserts:*[61]

> "You can't measure the ROI of social media! [Executives] expect social media to be as measurable as traditional marketing techniques, but you simply can't use the same metrics in this situation. You have to let go of the idea that you can measure dollar for dollar the return you get. People read tweets, but they don't always go out and buy. Sometimes it's about brand awareness, and after reading 20 tweets and seeing a company's logo on their friends' Facebook pages, they'll visit the website and buy."

This is wrong for a couple of reasons. First, a consumer can't follow a brand on social media that she isn't already aware of. So there goes the "awareness" rationale.

Second—and more importantly—is the reason why the "you can't measure the ROI" argument is wrong. If the majority of consumers who follow brands on social media do so for discounts and to purchase (per the IBM study), then sales, or revenue, is a perfectly valid measure of social media success.

There is another reason why ROI is a good metric (and why these social media gurus need to be quiet). It has to do with efficiency, not effectiveness.

Scenario: In 2010 a company did nothing social media-related. It spent $X on marketing, and achieved a Y% increase in sales, or customers, over the prior year. In 2011, it invested in social media, and at the end of the year, spent 10% less on marketing (because disseminating advertising messages or coupons through social media sites is less expensive than doing so through traditional media channels), and achieved a Y% increase in customers.

All other things being equal, the firm realized a positive ROI from social media. If social media is a lower cost channel than traditional channels, then even if it is no more effective than those traditional channels, the ROI on social media is positive.

[The problem with my example—which I'm well aware of, thank you—is that even though social media may be a lower cost channel, if marketing's budget goes up, the efficiency effect is more difficult to measure].

What's really screwy about the current marketing environment is that, on one hand, social media proponents argue that traditional channels are dead and social media channels are more effective for driving engagement and community (which presumably lead to stronger relationships as measured by retention and sales), but that, on the other hand, you can't measure the ROI of social media.

They can't have it both ways. You can—and should—measure the ROI of social media.

Not-So-Best Practices For Banks On Facebook

A Mashable article titled *5 Best Practices for Financial Institutions on Facebook* recommended that banks do the following on their Facebook pages: 1) Don't just talk about banking; 2) Host contests; 3) Offer career advice; 4) Be cool; and 5) Show off your good work.[62]

My take: To call something a "best practice" implies that it produces a positive, desirable business result. If you can't prove that it does, you need solid reasoning and logic why it should. Unfortunately, the Mashable article does neither.

Let's examine these so-called best practices one by one:

1. **Why shouldn't you just talk about banking?** People have a million places to go online to interact on the millions of things that occupy their time. Why in the world would they go to a bank or credit union Facebook page to watch a soccer video? It's not that it's wrong to talk about things other than banking (which I would broadly define as things related to managing one's financial life). But with the choices available, banks need to train customers to expect certain kinds of content on their Facebook page. Random content about non-banking things won't get people to come back often.

2. **Hosting a contest can't be bad, can it?** For most banks, hosting a contest on Facebook is like promising a friend you're going to take her to a great party, then driving out to some barren, deserted place, dropping her off and leaving. So you've lured your customer to your Facebook with the promise of winning a contest (which, if they had a brain in their head, they would know they wouldn't win), and then after they get there, you do nothing to keep them there, because the content on your Facebook is just a bunch of irrelevant drivel, rehashed from marketing messages dreamed up by some marketing intern. Nix the contests.

3. **Bank of America is where I always turn for career advice.** No better place to turn for career advice than to companies going through their own reductions-in-force. If you take career advice from a bank, or ask a bank for career advice, I hope I'm never stuck in the line at your cash register at Frenchy's Adult Book Store.

4. **Be cool.** Telling a bank to "be cool" is like telling Joe Biden to "be articulate." A bank does not qualify as cool just because it used the word "huzzah" on its Facebook page.

5. **Show off your good work.** I'm actually inclined to agree with this one. People who interact with their banks on

Facebook are highly engaged in their financial lives. They're not there to chit chat, watch soccer videos, or talk about whether or not they should quit their jobs. They're looking for a deeper connection with their chosen bank (I know that's hard to believe, but they are the minority), and want reinforcement that they've made the right decision about who to do business with. So go ahead and toot your horn from time to time.

Facebook Fans

Marketers who obsess over driving social media connections (like Facebook likes and Twitter follows) because they see or hear that social media likers/followers are more likely to buy, are better customers, or whatever, are missing an important point: Social media connections don't cause the desirable behavior/attitudes—they're the result of customer engagement.

Remember the engagement-based segmentation we looked at back in Chapter Four, where 20% of US consumers are Highly Active, 50% are Moderately Active, and 30% are Inactive?

Highly Active consumers are those most likely to connect with banks through social media. According to Aite Group's research, among Highly Active consumers, nearly 30% are Facebook fans of their primary FI, and 20% follow their bank on Twitter. Among other consumers, however, those percentages are in the low single digits.

Bottom line: Encouraging customers who aren't actively involved in the management of their financial lives to "Like us on Facebook!" or "Follow us on Twitter!" is a waste of financial services marketers' time and efforts. The customers who make those connections are already good customers.

Customer engagement—engagement with one's financial life—is what financial marketers should be encouraging.

Banks' Social Media Gender Challenge

Banks focusing on marketing to women, and intending to use social media to support those marketing efforts, have a problem. According to Aite Group, the majority of consumers that connect to their bank union through social media are men, not women.[63]

It's bad enough (if you're a believer in the marketing power of social media) that very few consumers connect to their banks through social media—11% have "liked" their bank's Facebook page, 6% follow their bank on Twitter, and 4% view their bank's YouTube videos. But, of those that do, most are men.

This means, of course, that banks' primary target—women—aren't connecting with their banks through social media. Among men, 9% follow their primary bank on Twitter compared to 4% of women. Six percent of men view banks' YouTube video, while just 2% of women do so. There's a little more parity regarding Facebook: 12% of men versus 10% of women.

In the broader context of the social media world, this is surprising. According to Digital Flash NYC:[64]

> "Women dominate both Facebook and Twitter, making up 58% and 64% of their memberships, respectively. Women use social media more frequently, with 18% of women updating their Facebook status on a daily basis, compared to 11% of men. On a monthly basis, women make 99 million more visits to social media sites than men; they're also more likely to comment on posts and photos several times a day."

Why aren't more women connecting to their banks through social media, in light of the fact that they dominate the financial decision-making in so many households?

My take: What women find on banks' social media sites and pages aren't of interest to them, and/or not helpful to them.

News of branch openings on Facebook pages doesn't engage women who make financial decisions. And maybe women just don't care about those amateurish videos bashing big banks that so many credit unions love to post on YouTube.

Bottom line: If banks want to use social media to improve their marketing efforts—and believe (as they should) that women are the key decision makers in the market—they've got a lot of work to do to attract and serve women on their social media offerings.

Integrating Social Media Into Marketing and Customer Service Processes

Is there a profitable and productive use for social media in banking? Yes, by integrating social concepts into existing channels. Banks can:

1. **Influence preferences.** America First Credit Union incorporates members' product reviews on the product pages. By doing this, the credit union accomplishes:

    *   **Customer advocacy.** Not just in the net promoter sense of the word—but in the more important sense of the word: Doing what's right for the customer and not just your own bottom line. Helping consumers make better choices—that are right for them—by enabling them to access other customers' opinions is a demonstration of customer advocacy.

    *   **Active engagement.** I guess that, if a customer follows you on Twitter and reads your tweets, or likes you on Facebook in order to enter a contest to win a prize, you could call that engagement. But I would call it passive engagement. Customers who take the time to post a review are more actively engaged, in my book.

- **Continuous market research.** I doubt many firms could capture the richness of information America First is capturing through satisfaction or net promoter surveys. And I know that they can't capture it in as timely a basis as America First does.

2. **Provide collaborative support.** Collaborative support is giving customers the opportunity to answer other customers' questions. Dell has been doing it for years. In the financial services arena, Mint.com used to do it. Why provide collaborative support?

    - **Reduced call volume.** I'm not going to say that you're going to see a huge volume of deflected calls, but over time, if you market the collaborative capability, it can help.

    - **Expanded knowledge base.** This is where the bigger value comes in. Customer service reps leverage internal knowledge bases to answer customer questions. Collaborative support helps grow that knowledge base, and helps figure out which answers and responses are more valuable than others. This expanded knowledge base will also prove valuable in training new employees.

    - **Active engagement.** Similar to the product reviews, customers who participate in collaborative support sites are demonstrating active engagement.

3. **Instill financial discipline.** According to Simone Baldassarri, writing on CollaborativeFinance.org:[65]

    "The idea behind social saving is that the more support you get in working towards your goals (especially in saving money) the more successful you can be. In terms of goal-setting, accountability does not need to be formal—just the fact that someone knows about my goal and will think poorly about me if I don't complete it is enough to encourage me. It's a relatively simple hack that can really increase your ability to move forward on your goals. That holds true for monetary goals just as much as any other ambition."

SmartyPig, for example, engages a consumer's community in the savings process by giving friends and family a way to contribute to the savings goal, and by making that savings goal public.

Social Versus Social Media

Ed Thompson, in a FutureLab article titled 3 *Ways Retail Banks Could Get More Benefit from Social Media*, offered banks ideas for how to use social media.[66] Or to be more precise, how banks can benefit from being more social—whether or not social media (like Facebook and Twitter) are used. Ed suggested that banks focus on:

"1. **Social banking.** Create a current or savings account with interest rates individually tailored to a customers' ability to recruit more members to the bank. New accounts could open with an average interest rate which increase by a small fraction each time a customer brought on a new member to join.

2. **Social micro-saving.** Create a savings account which encourages you to micro-save via your social platforms. This could also be used to encourage micro-donation to charities. This could work quite effectively as a Facebook app which occasionally puts something into a subscriber's news feed, reminding them to tuck £10 away in a savings account and make a small donation to charity.

3. **Social budget planning.** Mobile or social apps that let people compete over their personal budgeting targets could drive more careful budget planning and financial

prudence. If a couple, or group of friends, decided to collectively budget towards a savings target, they could opt in to share how well they were performing against self-imposed goals. Personal financial data would remain private, but benchmarking against targets for lunch-time spending, for example, could earn gamers reward points & bonuses, just in the same way that FourSquare currently awards players with badges and mayorships for check-in achievements."

My take: If banks want to engage their customers, they have to give customers a reason to engage. Mindless, idle chatter on Twitter and Facebook isn't sustainable. It will likely take years of experimentation to figure out what to say, when to say it, and how to say it on social media channels.

Bottom line: The path to making social media an important contributor to bottom line improvement—and sooner rather than later—will come from integration of social media concepts and approaches into everyday marketing and customer service processes.

Humor Break
Simplified Guide to Social Media Decision-Making

Does your company need a blog?

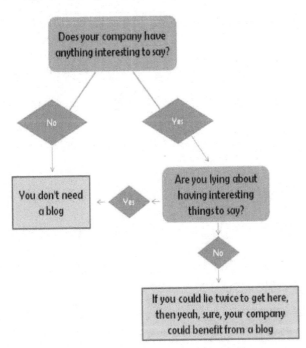

Does your company need a Twitter ID?

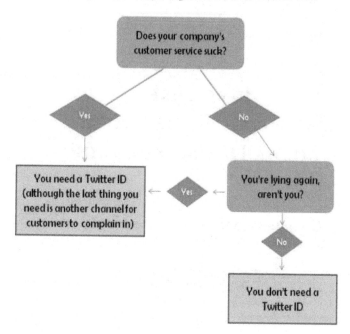

Chapter Fourteen
Big Data Delusions

In a creditunions.com article titled *Big Data At A Growing Credit Union*, an interview with a credit union executive went like this:[67]

"Q: Can you define Big Data?

A: Not really. But in a way, Big Data is what people have been doing all along—looking at and analyzing data. I don't know the tipping point where a credit union moves from generally looking at data and is suddenly in Big Data.

Q: Can't data also overwhelm and slow decisions?

A: It can unless you achieve the balance of talent and training. If you put the right data in the wrong hands you can be swimming in that data forever. You've got to get people to the point where they understand what's relevant and what's not, and that takes time.

Q: What do you feel is critical to success with Big Data?

A: You have to have directors and senior managers who are supportive and understand there are revelations this data can provide."

Pardon me if I can't help but think that this all sounds like a load of BS. If you can't define Big Data—other than saying it's what "people have been doing all along"—then how do you expect to get management support for it?

If you think Big Data represents a different way of managing your business, but you can't articulate that difference to your employees, you won't get broad employee support for the efforts.

Management is usually willing to fund some initiatives to try something promising. Employees, on the other hand, are generally loathe to change unless the pain of the existing is too much to bear. You might argue that they're willing to change if the potential upside is appealing enough, but I'm not so sure about that.

Jumping on the management fad bandwagon is a prescription for failure. It trains employees to put everything they want to get funding for under the fad banner, and diminishes whatever potential value really lies in the core of the new concept.

Avanade announced the results of a survey of more than 500 business executives and IT leaders, which revealed that:[68]

"The investments companies are making to manage big data are paying off. Eighty-four percent of respondents believe big data helps them make better business decisions. And 73% of companies have already used data to increase revenue by growing existing revenue streams (57%) or creating entirely new sources of revenue (43%). Evidence shows big data has become pervasive–more employees in businesses have greater access to increased technology options for managing and analyzing data."

According to the study:

"The benefits of big data come with meaningful challenges. Eighty-five percent of respondents report obstacles in managing and analyzing data, including being overwhelmed by sheer volume to data security concerns to not having enough dedicated staff to analyze the data. The majority of stakeholders (63%) also feel their company needs to develop new skills to turn data into business insights."

Oh really? These widespread challenges didn't seem to hinder the majority who think they're making better decisions and generating more revenue.

My take: This is complete and utter delusion.

The advent of Big Data is way-too-new for a majority of firms to: 1) have made investments; 2) have deployed solutions; and 3) have measured the impact of those investments, and then claim that they're making better decisions and creating new revenue streams.

Contrast the findings from this Avanade study to an eConsultancy study which found that only about one in three execs believe that web analytics, analyzing social media comments, or analyzing customer surveys to be very effective in helping them discover problems or issues with the customer experience.

If these approaches aren't that effective, then what exactly are respondents to the Avanade survey doing differently to make such great decisions and drive up revenue?

The real problem here is the lack of definition for Big Data.

I don't doubt that "more employees in businesses have greater access to increased technology options for managing and analyzing data." But how is that Big Data? Maybe what many of those employees are accessing is Little Data, or Medium Data.

Bottom line: Misuse of the term Big Data has become so pervasive that it practically renders the concept meaningless.

You Can't Get There From Here

Never mind, of course, that no one is willing to agree on exactly what Big Data is or isn't. Consider this comment on Enhanced Editions' website:[69]

> "Publishers have no insight into the effectiveness of their marketing. We firmly believe the answer to this problem lies in "big data"–that publishing can dramatically improve its return on marketing investment through the methodical analysis of campaigns, in combination with more agile marketing techniques."

Apparently, Big Data = Analytics. Who knew?

This is hardly an isolated example.

Personally, I think of Big Data as data types and sources that are created via digital channels (online, mobile, etc.), as well as data that is created because so many devices (not just PCs, tablets, and cell phones, but cars, refrigerators, and whatever other mechanical devices are connected to the Internet and can become a source of data).

But I'm not here to impose my definition of Big Data on anyone. I don't care how you define it. I care about how banks are going to use the data in a way that improves the bank's effectiveness, efficiency, and profitability. In that context, there are a few hurdles that many Big Data advocates fail to recognize:

1. **More data will cause more problems, not less.** The ability to capture people's online behavior adds a lot of data to the marketing arsenal. And there is a lot of discussion about how "unstructured" data—e.g., conversational data—that occurs in social media channels can be captured and analyzed. But unstructured or not, the act of capturing data requires us to label and categorize it — that is, to define it. The act of defining data opens the door for differences and errors in interpretation.

Example: Assume that a scanner can sense when a customer goes into a store, and record it as a "store visit."

Wouldn't it be great for retailers to know how many of their customers visited a store, when, and for how long? Reconciling with a transaction system can help determine if a sale was made during a particular visit, and if not, perhaps signal the retailer to send a marketing message to the effect "Couldn't find what you were looking for? Maybe we can help!"

But what if that store was in a mall. And what if my reason for being in the store was simply that the parking spot I found was close to the store. Oh sure, maybe your "inter-action system" (in contrast to your "transaction system") will disregard short visits. But right off the bat, we've introduced two decisions that have to be made about our new "big data": What exactly is a "store visit" and "how long does a visit have to be to be considered a store visit."

Now multiply these decisions by the multitudes of data sources and data types that Big Data advocates rant and rave about. I think we've exceeded humans' data processing capacity.

Aha, but no worry, the Big Data advocates say, that's what the technology is for. Which takes me to the second big Big Data hurdle…

2. **Data won't analyze itself.** I've worked for a database marketing company. You know who does the analysis? Really smart people with PhDs in statistics.

Your company likely has one, maybe two problems. Number one, you might not have a lot of smart people. That's your subjective call (I have my opinion, but sharing it will only make people think I'm cranky and elitist).

The more likely case is that your firm doesn't have a lot of Statistics PhDs on staff.

The Big Data advocates know this, and assure us that our schools will turn out kids whose knowledge of statistics is far greater than it is today. Okey dokey.

But let me share a secret about today's Statistics PhDs that they won't be happy that I'm sharing: They don't know how to incorporate new data sources. Let me restate this in a more positive way: They're still learning how to incorporate new data sources.

The purchase propensity models that they've developed use the data that's available today, which, I guess for lack of a better term, could be considered Little Data. Little Data is predominantly demographic and purchase (i.e., transaction) data, not behavioral and conversational data.

What many Big Data advocates don't seem to understand is that when you've developed and tested a propensity model in the real world, making changes to that model (because you have some "new" data) is a risky, and potentially expensive endeavor.

Database marketers like to test new data sources before making big investments in the capture, storing, and utilization of that data for marketing purposes.

How is all this going to happen in the Big Data advocates' vision of Big Data Nirvana? Who's going to do all of this?

No worries, say the Big Data advocates. Companies will start hiring more Data Scientists (the more adventurous of which will call themselves "Data Whisperers" causing me to barf my lunch). If you believe this, you need to read on to the third hurdle...

3. **The cultural hurdles will be tough to overcome.** How many Data Scientists do you think the marketing department of a large retailer or financial services firm is going to hire? Database marketing can't get the budget to increase its staff today, how is this magically going to change in the near future? Oh, these Data Scientists are going to reside in IT, which charges back its expenses to the rest of the organization, and is under constant cost pressure?

The budget issue isn't even the biggest of the cultural hurdles.

Here's the problem, and nobody wants to admit it: The CEO or CFO can look at a TV ad and say "I love it" or "I hate it." They can't look at a propensity model and say "I'm not crazy about that model."

Organizations are typically run by people with years of experience in that industry and/or that firm. They develop beliefs about what works and what doesn't. Ceding decision making power to the "data" or the "analytics" requires a leap of faith that is typically only found in firms on burning platforms, or in Brad Pitt movies.

Now don't get me wrong—if Hollywood wants to turn this book into a movie, I'd be more than happy to have Brad Pitt play me in the movie. But in the Big Data advocates' view of the world, their envisioned future is fantasy, not science fiction.

There are some major hurdles in the way of Big Data having the impact that advocates envision it to have. And, I'm not very confident that many companies—as they say in Maine—can get there from here.

At least not in the short-term. Because I do believe that the ability to capture and analyze behavioral and conversational data will transform marketing. But I think it's going to take 25 to 30 years before we really see marketing departments with strong competencies in Big Data analysis. OK, maybe 20.

And I really don't care if I'm off by a few years or not, because I hope to be retired in Maine by then. And no, you can't come visit me—because you can't get there from here.

CHAPTER FIFTEEN
THE MOBILE WALLET
OPPORTUNITY

comScore conducted a study regarding consumers' awareness of mobile wallets, and found that nearly half of all consumers (assuming the study surveyed a representative set of consumers) have used PayPal's digital wallet.[70] That would mean that pretty much everybody in the US who owns a smartphone has used PayPal's digital wallet (Table 15.1).

Table 15.1

Digital Wallet	Percentage of respondents aware of digital wallet	Percentage of respondents who used the digital wallet
PayPal	72%	48%
Google Wallet	41%	8%
MasterCard PayPass	13%	3%
Square Wallet	8%	2%
V.me by Visa	8%	2%
ISIS	6%	1%
Lemon Wallet	5%	1%
LevelUp	5%	2%

Source: comScore Digital Wallet Road Map 2013

I can hear the PayPal people laughing at that all the way here on the other side of the continent.

I find it funny, too, because, until recently, PayPal didn't even have a digital wallet. According to articles published in March 2012, May 2012 was the expected launch date for the PayPal digital wallet, however, I can't find any articles that confirm that it was launched then.

Well, hold on a second here. Maybe our terminology isn't accurate. Maybe PayPal has a digital wallet, but not a mobile wallet. Yes, that must be it.

But if that's the case, then one-click buying on Amazon is a digital wallet, too. And since you can make P2P transactions from many banks' online banking platforms, that's kind of a digital wallet, too, no? But comScore didn't ask about the awareness of either of those wallets.

If you're confused about the difference between a digital and mobile wallet, or what a mobile wallet exactly is, welcome to the club. According to the comScore study, less than half of the respondents said they really understand what a digital wallet is (then how can we trust them when they say they're aware of a vendor's digital wallet, or that they've used it?).

Let's take a look at some of the other numbers.

According to the comScore study, 1% of respondents use (or have used) the Lemon Wallet and 2% use LevelUp. The companies, themselves, report quite different numbers.

A Mobile Commerce Today article from December 2012 stated that LevelUp had reached the 500k user mark. Meanwhile, a Bank Systems & Technology article from November 2012 said that Lemon Wallet had 2.5 million users.

My calculator says the number of Lemon Wallet users are five times larger than the number of LevelUp users. Yet the comScore study reports that LevelUp's market penetration is double that of Lemon's. Maybe my calculator is broken.

What should we make of all this?

Simply, that the mobile wallet space is one messy pile of you-know-what at the moment, and that any claim about who's winning or losing is: 1) bogus, and 2) the work of a fool.

What's the Value Proposition with Mobile Wallets?

A Finextra study of banks' mobile wallet plans found that:[71]

> "81% of banks are looking to add value beyond the transaction, including providing relevant offers to consumers at the point of sale."

My take: Add value to whom? To consumers? Really? You've got research that shows consumers want more offers thrown at them?

Does your research also show that consumers want to walk down a busy city street and have offers pop up on their mobile devices as they approach every store on the block?

Oh, I see...your research shows that consumers want "more relevant" offers.

Good luck with that. Relevance is a slippery notion. Many marketers suffer from delusions of relevance. Relevance can't be quantified or measured—it's a subjective, and transient condition.

If the marketers who sell a particular product can't figure out what's relevant to a particular consumer, how is a banker supposed to figure it out?

Oh, I see...you say it's about providing relevant offers at the point of sale?

So when I'm at the register at Starbucks paying for my Venti Skinny Half-Caf Ristretto Macchiato-style Americano, you're going to hit me with an offer for a large coffee at Dunkin' Donuts? Or did you mean that you'll offer me a nickel off a muffin (right after the barista, who knows me cuz' I'm there 10 times a week, offers me the muffin he knows I always get)?

If you thought that the financial crisis brought bankers to their senses, you were wrong. Turns out that many still live in la-la-land.

If they think that consumers will adopt their mobile wallets, and use them to make mobile payments because of the "value-added" of receiving offers, I have ocean-front property in Kansas to sell them.

The "value" in providing offers through mobile wallets (and at the point of sale during a mobile payment) isn't to consumers, but to merchants and retailers. It's the promise of helping them reach prospects (or even customers more efficiently and effectively than they do today.

What consumers want is to have their bank (through a mechanism like a mobile wallet) limit, or filter, the number of offers they receive. That's what consumers really want. Not more, but less offers. Somebody to intercept the offer and figure out "oh no, not another offer from a nail salon—that's the last thing Ron needs!"

But who's going to pay for that? Consumers aren't going to pay banks to get fewer, albeit more relevant, offers. It's not clear that consumers really want to pay banks for anything (and if banks do charge for something, you can be sure Dick Durbin will come running in screaming for regulatory action).

The value proposition of the traditional checking account was "a safe and convenient place to park your money until you needed it." The rise of the debit card was fueled by a value proposition that promised "a more convenient way to make a payment."

The value proposition of the so-called mobile wallet—whatever that means, considering there's no consensus on its definition—isn't clear just yet. I wouldn't bet my money on it being "an even more convenient way to make a payment." And I wouldn't bet on it being "a way to get more relevant offers."

No, my money is on "helping consumers make smarter decisions about their finances and spending." (This is why the new basis of competition is performance).

The question that bankers should be addressing is "how do we help our customers make better decisions?", and not "what should we put in our mobile wallet if we build one?"

Mobile Wallets and the Convenience Factor

Much of the discussion regarding the adoption of mobile wallets involves whether or not they provide an added level of convenience for consumers. Writing in American Banker, Daniel Wolfe says:[72]

> "Convenience is a tired selling point for mobile wallets. The argument goes that tapping a contactless card or payment-capable phone against a special reader is so much easier and faster than swiping a card that a consumer would be eager to change their habits. In reality, most people, of course, don't consider plastic cards all that time-consuming. Checks and cash may take a little more time than cards, but not enough to make most people demand some kind of relief."

My take: The industry needs to redefine its perspective on mobile wallets' convenience.

Wolfe is right that swiping a plastic card isn't all that time-consuming. And even if checks and cash do take longer, let's get real here: The heavy check writers are not the people who will be adopting mobile wallets because of its promise of added convenience.

But I disagree with the point regarding mobile wallets' selling point. Convenience is not a tired selling point. In fact, more broadly speaking, added convenience is usually the best selling point—or reason for adoption—for new technological innovations.

The problem with the mobile wallet convenience story is that many people don't look at it broadly enough. The real added convenience for mobile wallets isn't at the point of tender transfer (I'm trying to avoid saying "point of transaction" because there are multiple steps in the transaction process, of which "tender transfer" is one). Mobile wallets will prove out their convenience as they help consumers manage:

1) **Receipts.** Even though swiping a card is fast and easy, credit and debit transactions still produce a paper receipt. And if that transaction occurs at a Staples, Best Buy, or CVS, it produces about three pounds of paper receipts.

There is a growing segment of the population that wants to go paperless—not just for monthly bills and statements, but—for everything. It's not a "green" thing. It's a convenience thing. Managing all this paper is a huge hassle.

When I travel, after making a reimbursable purchase, I take a picture of the receipt, email it to my expense tracking app, and throw the piece of paper away (on the ground, of course, because I don't want to be accused of being a Green-weenie).

2) **Reward points.** Reward redemption is a real pain-in-the-you-know-what. Redeeming rewards at the point of sale using mobile wallets will become a key impetus to change consumers' behavior.

3) **Coupons.** Is there anything more 1980 than seeing someone in the supermarket scanning a ton of coupons at the register? Eventually, even the least-likely candidate to adopt mobile wallets will recognize that the technology's ability to store and use digital coupons is more convenient than what they do today.

4) **Gift cards.** As businesses increasingly issue refunds, rebates, and rewards on gift cards, and as these cards

increasingly replace cash gifts, the number of cards consumers have really add up. Keeping track of them through mobile wallets will prove to be a huge convenience for consumers.

One last question to consider: Why is the industry's view of mobile wallet convenience so limited? I have a theory, and it has to do with organizational structure.

In many banks and card issuers, mobile payment (and wallet) initiatives are still led by, and perhaps even limited to, the payments group. What that means is that marketing's, and maybe even the online channel group's, level of involvement is limited.

No offense to the payments people, but I find that their focus is often limited to the payments transaction and how it's processed and cleared. And not on how it impacts consumers.

Merchants' Mobile Wallet: The MCX Consortia

Google, Apple, and banks aren't the only ones looking to get into the mobile wallet game. Merchants are tired of paying a 0.8% fee on debit card transactions, and have formed a consortium (named MCX) to be a mobile-only payments network which will give consumers "access to a personalized payment experience integrated with merchant offers, promotions, loyalty and location-based services, which they will be able to use at many of the large retailers at which they regularly shop." Completely understandable.

But can a mobile wallet from a consortium of merchants succeed? Judging from my estimates of the costs and benefits of a merchant-issued mobile wallet, the prospects are dim.

Cornerstone Advisors, a leading consultancy in the financial services industry, surveyed consumers and found that merchants, in order to get consumers to make mobile payments, will need to offer some kind of incentive (i.e., a discount).

In addition, MCX members will pay a transaction fee to FIS for processing transactions and some amount of money to Gemalto for the development of the mobile wallet/payment app.

And in order to drive awareness and adoption of a mobile payments apps, merchants will need to run some kind of advertising campaign. (If you build it, they will come? I think not).

I've run a few scenarios with alternative assumptions. In the most optimistic (for merchants) scenario, merchants cut their transaction costs by a little more than half. In the least optimistic scenario, their costs are nearly six times higher than they are with the current interchange rate structure. Even the moderate scenario, however, has transaction costs more than twice as high as the current level.

FIS' processing costs will come in between 0.05% and 0.10% of the transaction value per transaction, about 1/8th to 1/16th of the current interchange fee. An estimate of $100k to $200k for Gemalto's fee is probably too low, but better to err on the cautious side.

To get consumers to use the mobile payment app, as the research shows, merchants will need to offer a discount—especially to get consumers to do the first mobile transaction. So anywhere from 1% of 5% of transactions will need to offer a discount. With the average debit card transaction coming to just shy of $30, a discount of $0,25 or $0,50 is probably too low to be an effective incentive, but I'll give the merchants the benefit of the doubt here.

Merchants will have to launch an advertising campaign to make consumers aware of this, and get them to download and use the app. That's got to cost at least $250k, and my high estimate of $500k is probably too low.

The key variable? Discounts. If merchants can drive adoption of their mobile wallet without a big incentive, then the move pays off. If large discounts are required, the business case goes down the tank (Table 15.2).

Table 15.2

	Scenarios			
	Baseline	**Optimistic**	**Moderate**	**Pessimistic**
Total debit transactions	15,600,000,000	15,600,000,000	15,600,000,000	15,600,000,000
% mobile debit transactions	2.5%	5.0%	3.0%	2.0%
# of transactions	390,000,000	780,000,000	468,000,000	312,000,000
Processing (interchange) fee per transaction	0.80%	0.05%	0.10%	0.10%
Processing fees	$3,120,000	$390,000	$468,000	$312,000
Mobile app development fee	$0	$100,000	$200,000	$500,000
% of transactions w/ discount	0%	1%	3%	5%
Average discount per transaction	$0	$0.25	$0.50	$1.00
Total discount costs	$0	$1,950,000	$7,020,000	$15,600,000
Advertising costs	$0	$250,000	$500,000	$1,000,000
Total costs	$3,120,000	$2,690,000	$8,188,000	$17,412,000
Total cost % of transaction	0.8%	0.3%	1.7%	5.6%

The consortia's digital wallet won't pay off for merchants because:

1) **Consumers show a willingness to use a mobile wallet from a preferred vendor.** Case in point: Starbucks. A mobile wallet from a consortium of merchants? Eh.

2) **Consortia are tough to pull off.** Too many conflicting interests. There's one player, in particular, in the mix who tends to not play well in the multi-merchant sandbox.

3) **Current interest in mobile wallets among consumers is low.** Mostly due to the fact that few people have any clue what a "mobile wallet" really is. There's little doubt that awareness and interest will grow, but the two previous factors—consumers' desire to use individual merchants' wallets and the difficulty keeping a consortium together for any length of time—will make it difficult for MCX participants to stick with the group for any length of time, waiting for consumer demand to catch up.

Banks' Mobile Wallet Opportunity

An analyst with a leading technology analyst firm wrote:[73]

"Banks should think twice before going down the path of launching their own branded independent wallets. For some, it might make sense, but many others will likely be better off focusing on making their payment credentials available and top of wallet in the wallets already out in the market, as well as enhancing and extending their mobile banking platforms with value-added services, including payments."

My take: Nothing could be farther from the truth. Mobile wallets are key to transforming banking, and repairing the bank/customer relationship.

Banks do provide value to their customers. They provide security, and a guarantee that money will be moved when it's supposed to be, and there in the account when it's supposed to be.

In the scheme of things, however, these are low on the Maslow hierarchy of banking value. People want added convenience to do the things they do, and help making better financial decisions, big and little. That's the promise of a digital wallet—convenience and advice. If banks don't brand their own digital wallets, someone else will—and deliver more value to consumers. I didn't say that every bank had to build their own digital wallet. But providing and branding their own wallet will be a big battlefield over the next few years.

Some people believe the mobile wallet opportunity lies in the delivery of offers. Listen to David Marcus, former president of PayPal:[74]

> "It's about providing an entire shopping experience and ensuring people get relevant offers for what they are buying. And that doesn't happen unless you have data."

The points about the shopping experience and having data are spot on. But people don't care about getting "relevant offers." That's marketing-speak.

The notion of relevance is misunderstood. Marketers have delusions of relevance. Relevance can't be quantified (and therefore not measured). It's a highly subjective and transient condition.

Delusions of Relevance

At a conference I recently attended, the CEO of a large telco said:[75]

> "Our value proposition—to both content providers and consumers—is added relevance. We won't promise to our

customers that they'll see less advertising—but what we promise is that what they do see will be relevant."

In another session, a senior exec with a payments-related company commented:

"Payments data will be used to ensure that merchants' offers are relevant."

My take: Marketers are deluding themselves about the notion of relevance. The problem—which no one wants to admit—is that relevance can't be quantified (and therefore not measured). It's a highly subjective, and worse, transient condition.

Hypothetical example #1: Before going on vacation last year, I clicked on numerous banner ads for hotels in Sedona, AZ. Marketing logic would have it that showing me another ad for hotels in Sedona would make sense under the banner of relevance. But once I make my choice of hotels, the window of relevance closes down. At some point, a threshold is reached in which one more ad or offer crosses the line from relevant to irrelevant.

Hypothetical example #2: I eat cereal (almost) every day. Analyzing my payments stream (assuming SKU level data was available) would suggest that: 1) I have an unhealthy obsession with cereal, and 2) cereal ads would be relevant to me. Nothing could be further from the truth. I can quit my cereal habit any time I want, and I have absolutely no desire to see cereal advertising. Cereal makers might want me to see their ads, but that's relevance to them as marketer, not to me as a consumer.

Hypothetical example #3: Nobody knows this, but when I'm done with this analyst gig my next career will be in the music field—I'm going to be the guitarist in a Grateful Dead cover band. (Never mind the small fact that I can't play guitar worth a damn, and that my singing has been known to cause headaches and ear pain). I'm already dreaming about the guitar equipment I'm going to buy. For me, ads and offers for guitars would be highly relevant. Of course, nothing in my current behavior gives marketers any clue to this.

I could identify 100 hypothetical examples to prove that what marketers think are "relevant" offers or ads, may, in fact, be totally irrelevant from the consumer perspective.

We could ask consumers "How relevant were the offers you received [today/this week/this month] from [one-of-the-thousand-of-providers-they-get-offers-from]?"

But the subjectivity of the answer would prove the results useless, as would the fact that consumers' ability to recall what offers they received, or which ads they were shown, by any particular provider is slim.

Bottom line: Achieving relevance in offers and ads is a delusion. At least as it applies to the consumer (or as some might put it, from the "consumer-centric" view).

Marketers don't care—and there is a case to be made that they shouldn't care—about whether or not consumers view their offers and ads as relevant. If they're spending money to put an offer or ad in front of a consumer, then what matters is whether or not that prospect or customer is relevant to them— and not whether or not they think the consumer will find the ad/offer relevant.

This might seem like I'm mincing words. After all, if the consumer doesn't find the offer relevant s/he won't look at it, right? But the problem is that predicting what a consumer finds relevant based on prior behavior and attitudes is unreliable.

The end result is that we shouldn't expect to see any decline in the number of offers/ads shown to consumers, and that their view that what they see isn't relevant is unlikely to change, as well.

Making Mobile Offers

People don't really want more offers.

BuyVia, an app/website that claims to be the first all-in-one smart shopping experience across devices (whatever that means), conducted a consumer survey which found "the majority (56%) of shoppers want to be notified of deals via push notifications on their mobile devices when in an area with local deals."[76]

Oh really?

As a wannabe legitimate market researcher, I would never publish research results based on an insufficient sample, but from time to time I use my wife and/or daughters as sanity checks (which is ironic, since I usually blame them for my insanity).

I asked my wife: "Do you want to be notified of deals via push notifications on your Blackberry when you're in an area with local deals?"

The look on her face said "What are you talking about?" but her mouth said "What's a push notification, and how would I know if I was in an area with a local deal? What does that mean?"

I could ask 1,000 consumers the same question I asked my wife to get their responses and see if the answers differ from my wife's. But I've already asked consumers about their interest in receiving offers, and the results I got don't jive with BuyVia's.

Aite Group asked US consumers: "how important is it to you to receive special offers from merchants on your mobile device when shopping?" Just 14% said "very important," 27% said "somewhat important," and 60% said "not very important." By generation, a not-so-whopping 23% of Gen Yers, 17% of Gen Xers, 8% of Boomers, and 0.6% of Seniors replied "very important."

From this, I'd find it hard to conclude that "the majority of shoppers want to be notified of deals via push notifications on their mobile devices when in an area with local deals." Maybe BuyVia was only considering younger consumers to be "shoppers." After all, us old people (Boomers, Seniors) don't really matter anymore, do we?

Why don't consumers want offers pushed to them? If you think it's because consumers see advertising as a nuisance and a disruption, I agree. But there is another reason: Data privacy.

Aite Group also asked consumers about their willingness to share various types of personal data with merchants and retailers in order for that data to be used to personalize offers. For the various types of sources, consumers were asked to what extent they have reservations about merchants using their personal information. The generational differences are significant (Table 15.3):

Table 15.3

Percentage of consumers that say that merchants should not access
information from the following sources under any circumstances

Source	Gen Y	Gen X	Boomer	Senior
Current search	28%	40%	51%	65%
Retail purchase history	28%	44%	55%	66%
Search history	29%	44%	55%	70%
Purchase history (from FI)	32%	48%	56%	71%
Location information	33%	44%	56%	73%
Payment information	35%	47%	60%	73%
Social media profiles/posts	35%	46%	62%	74%
Web browsing history	35%	47%	56%	74%
Banks account balances	40%	56%	67%	85%

Source: Aite Group

Still think that the "majority" of consumers want offers
pushed to them?

The truth is not as simple as "consumers want mobile offers"
or "consumers don't want mobile offers." We want offers to
magically appear when we want them to, which can be at any
point in the purchase decision process. That point differs by
person, and differs for even a particular consumer based on
product, mood, and a million other factors.

We say we don't want merchants/retailers to use our personal
data, but then complain when they don't "know" us.

The reality is that some subset of consumers are OK with
offers pushed to their mobile device, and having some subset
of their personal data used to personalize that offer.

The best marketers can do is figure out which customers
and prospects are in that subset, and what they can do to grow
the segment. In the meantime, don't believe claims like "the
majority of consumers want to be notified of deals via push

notifications on their mobile devices when in an area with local deals."

People care about getting the best price for what they're buying, and choosing the best product for them when there's a choice. That's the shopping experience. If a better price is available somewhere, people want to know. If the digital wallet offers them the ability to find the better price, then people will use the digital wallet.

The question is: How does that "better price" get into the digital wallet? It could come from price comparison functionality with the mobile wallet. Or another company could make an offer to match or better the price of a product you're looking at (similar to the bidding that occurs on Google.com with search results).

It's unlikely that the MCX wallet will contain competing offers from companies that aren't part of the consortium. There goes getting a wide variety of choices in that mobile wallet.

It's up to banks to develop and provide this capability. It's how they will prove their value. Customers will pay for this kind of capability when they see the money they save.

The question that banks need to answer is simple (not that there is a simple answer): Where in the mobile customer experience do banks add value?

Take a look at the picture below (Figure 15.1):

Figure 15.1

Let's say that a consumer scans the bar code or QR code for a pair of shoes. There are plenty of apps on the marketplace that can tell the customer it's a pair of Jimmy Choo shoes that cost US$400 (not that you can really get Jimmy Choo shoes for US$400, but play along for a moment). There are not, however, apps available that address the following questions:

- **Can the customer afford the shoes?** Being able to answer this question requires the app to access the customer's bank and credit card accounts, and have some knowledge of the upcoming inflows and outflows associated with those accounts. Google, Apple, and the MCX consortia participants can't access that information. Only banks can do that.

- **How should the customer pay?** I've got three daughters who probably don't care about the first question since Daddy is paying for the shoes. Hopefully, if they're out shopping, they'll think about this second question. Should a customer put a purchase on her debit card or one of her credit cards? Can she use rewards points earned towards the purchase?

- **Can the customer get an offer?** Is there another merchant (maybe one within a certain geographic distance) willing to match or better this price?

- **What did others pay?** Is this a good deal? How does it compare with what other people paid for the product?

- **What do others think?** How good or bad are the reviews for this product?

Few banks understand that mobile shopping is the link between mobile banking and mobile payments. In the new world of mobile shopping, banks must figure out how to add value in this process beyond "checking balances" prior to the transaction, and being the "payment mechanism" (mobile device or not) at the culmination of the transaction.

Consumers don't buy homes or cars very frequently. Most don't even make investment-related decisions very often (if at all). But we all spend money on a nearly daily basis. Helping consumers make smarter decisions about how they spend their money (and how they should pay for those purchases) will emerge as the new value proposition in retail banking.

The Mobile Moments of Opportunity

The mobile wallet space is in a period of constant evolution. Devolution may be the better word.

Square's Wallet is off the market (if you consider the Apple Store to be the market, that is). Visa's v.me is off the market (if you consider the US to be the market, that is). Lifelock's mobile wallet is off the market (regardless of how you define the market).

On the other hand, Amazon launched its mobile wallet (if you consider a "beta" version to be a product launch, and if you consider what they did launch to be a "mobile wallet").

Initial reviews have not been particularly complimentary. TechCrunch called it a "quiet debut." Michael Dudas, a payments executive formerly with Venmo, Google and PayPal, tweeted "Amazon released a joke of a mobile wallet product today." His beef with the product (expressed in a public tweet) was that "it only stores digital versions of loyalty & gift cards, there's zero payment functionality."

Bank Innovation, a leading financial services publication, tweeted, "the app does not (yet) have the ability to store credit and debit cards, which seems to be integral for a mobile wallet." That's the essence of the issue here: What is a mobile wallet, and what, exactly is "integral"?

Regardless of how you define mobile wallets, or what is or isn't integral, some of the consumer data regarding the concept is perplexing. According to a Media Post article:[77]

" While most consumers (78%) are aware of digital wallets, only about a third (32%) has ever used them, according to the 2014 Digital Wallet Usage Study by Thrive Analytics."

Let's do some math here. As of mid-2014, roughly two-thirds of mobile phone subscribers in the United States (who comprise about 85% of consumers) have a smartphone. That means about 56% of all consumers have a smartphone. If one-third of all consumers have used a digital wallet, then more than half (~57%) of all smartphone owners have used a mobile wallet, if the Thrive study is correct.

But I don't think it is. That percentage seems way too high. Maybe the Thrive study's numbers refer to percentages of smartphone owners, not all consumers (note to Media Post: That's kind of an important distinction).

The Thrive study also found that, among mobile wallet users (however many of them there are), just one-third used a mobile wallet at least on a weekly basis, and just 7% used it daily.

So, regardless of how many mobile wallet users there really are (and I would argue there really aren't very many)–and regardless of what is and isn't "integral" to the wallet–digital wallets have hardly become an integral part of consumers' daily lives.

Why not?

Data points of one are dangerous, but when I ask my wife–a baby boomer who manages the family's finances–about her interest in mobile wallets, her response is: "What's a mobile wallet? What I really need is something to keep track of all the damned gift card and prepaid cards we have. I hate carrying those things around, and when I do, I have no idea how much money is on them."

Dudas' critique of Amazon's mobile wallet—"there's zero payment functionality"--represents a data point of one, as well. Neither Mike's nor my wife's opinions of mobile wallets are right or wrong. They simply point to the varied needs of (potentially) different segments of consumers. The question is: Which segment is bigger, and will drive the market for digital wallets?

My take: Making the payment is not the part of the customer experience that consumers want a digital wallet (whatever that might be) to improve. The mobile moments of opportunity–to improve the customer experience, to add new levels of convenience to the customer experience, to help consumers make better/smarter decisions about how they manage and spend their money–occur before and after the payment.

That is, the mobile moments of opportunity come during consumers' decision-making process, and in the tracking and analysis of their spending post-payment.

In the course of the shopping or purchasing experience, before the actual payment transaction, consumers want to know:

1) **Is this the right product for me?** That's why 40% of smartphone owners scan labels and UPC codes in the store while shopping.

2) **Is this the best price I can get?** That's why about a third of smartphones store coupons on their mobile device.

3) **How can/should I pay for this?** Would putting this on my Amex credit card be better than paying for it with my debit card or some other credit card I have? Do I have rewards points I can apply to the purchase?

After the payment transaction, consumers want to know:

1) **How much did they spend on a particular category of product so far this month?** Haha, just kidding. Nobody really cares about that. OK, seriously, just kidding about kidding. The history of PFM adoption would suggest that not a lot of people care about this question. I would argue, however, that the low adoption is more a function of the shortcomings of online PFM than a function of low interest on the part of consumers. As mobile PFM evolves, we'll see more interest in this question.

2) **Where are all those receipts for all those products I purchased?** That's why about a quarter of smartphone owners scan paper receipts into their smartphone (source: Aite Group). (I always feel bad for those consumers who

do that who shop at CVS–it must take them an hour to scan the receipt from just one visit).

A wallet is nothing more than a receptacle to hold things. In modern society, a wallet has evolved to hold things we make payments with. Most people, however, keep other things–photos, drivers license, pictures of their kids–in their wallets, as well. So a wallet doesn't have to be just for enabling payments. Shouldn't that logic apply to digital wallets, as well?

There are three factors that influence consumers to change their behavior: Faster, cheaper, better.

Using a mobile wallet to simply make a payment might be faster, but I doubt many consumers see a big difference. And cheaper and better don't factor in.

Cheaper and better come from functionality that surround the payment.

Bottom line: In the long run, the concept of a digital wallet won't last. The smartphone is the mobile wallet. The smartphone is the receptacle that holds all the functionality–pictures, personal identification, payment mechanisms–that today's (non-digital, I probably shouldn't call them non-mobile, because they are mobile) wallets provide.

The mobile moments of opportunity come from providing capabilities that go beyond simply digitizing the existing set of capabilities.

CHAPTER SIXTEEN
THE MOBILE FINANCE APPS
OPPORTUNITY

A quick peek into Apple's iTunes Apps Store reveals more than 1,600 Finance-related apps that begin with the letter A. I wasn't about to count them all, but I'd estimate there is about 25,000 finance-related apps in the Apps Store.

If you're a consumer looking for an app to help you manage your financial life, good luck. You can get a list of the most popular apps, but most of them are bank-specific, so if you're not a customer of the bank, you probably don't want that app.

You can see ratings for the apps, but only by clicking on the link for the app. Call me when you've gone through all 25,000 apps.

My take: Competing on performance means banks must help consumers find (and integrate) the right apps for customers' specific financial needs. In essence, banks will create their own "apps store" to sell and distribute mobile apps from a variety of providers, and not just the ones they develop themselves.

Financial Apps Loyalty

There's no denying that consumers have shifted their online behavior from the PC to mobile devices. But the behavioral shift isn't just about change of device. It's a shift from browser to apps. As Flurry Analytics reported in April 2013 (Figure 16.1):[78]

"The U.S. consumer spends an average of 2 hours and 38 minutes per day on smartphones and tablets. 80% of that time is spent inside apps and 20% is spent on the mobile web. Gaming apps remain the largest category of all apps with 32% of time spent."

Figure 16.1

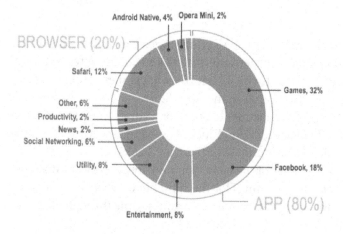

Time Spent on iOS & Android Connected Devices

Source: Flurry Analytics, comScore, NetMarketShare

From 2010 to 2012, as the average minutes per day of TV consumption increased by just 4% from 162 minutes to 168 minutes, time spent on mobile apps nearly doubled from 66 minutes to 127 minutes (Figure 16.2).

Figure 16.2

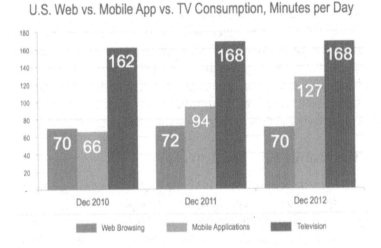

U.S. Web vs. Mobile App vs. TV Consumption, Minutes per Day

Source: *Flurry Analytics, comScore, Alexa, US Bureau of Labor Statistics*

By October 2013, apps had been downloaded from Apple's iTunes store 60 billion times. And that was up from 50 billion announced just five months earlier. In January 2012, Nielsen reported that 30% of smartphone and tablet owners had downloaded at least one banking/finance app in the 30 days prior to the survey.[79] The category with the highest percentage of smartphone/tablet owners downloading an app was games, at 68%.

Mobile analytics company Flurry measures app loyalty by looking at two factors: 1) How many hours per week users use the mobile app, and 2) How long users keep an app on their mobile device.

When the company measured loyalty in November 2012, users kept just 35% of apps on their device for at least 90 days, and used each app an average of 3.7 hours per week. Banking apps came in right about at the overall averages, averaging 36%

retention over 90 days, and 3.7 hours per week usage. Financial tools apps fared about the same on retention (35%), but a bit lower on usage (2.2 hours per week).

My take: These numbers will dramatically increase over the next few years. Why? As the most-frequent users of mobile apps—Gen Yers—get older, managing their finances will become much more important that it is today. As a result, they'll shift their mobile apps behavior (even if only slightly) from playing games to managing their money.

The Mobile Finance Apps Hub

Where is the opportunity for banks? It's in becoming a financial apps hub (i.e., apps store, or marketplace) for consumers. Not only will banking customers need help in finding, vetting, and integrating financial-related apps, but the developers of apps desperately need help reaching prospective customers. According to Tim Shepherd, an analyst at market research firm Canalys:[80]

> "When we speak with app developers, many are concerned about monetization or platform fragmentation, but the number one problem they face is getting their apps noticed."

With a large base of customers, banks are in a position to help apps developers. The revenue opportunity for banks is threefold: 1) Direct revenue from the sale of apps; 2) Revenue share from in-app purchases made through partner apps; and 3) Product sales from in-app purchases.

Banks won't see a lot of revenue from the first path. Research firm Distimo estimated that paid apps accounted for 24% of all apps-related revenue in February 2013 (in-app purchases through free apps accounted for 71% of revenue, and in-app purchases through paid apps amounted to 5% of the total).

For the past few years, however, paid apps' percentage of total revenue generated has steadily declined. Unfortunately—from a banking perspective—just 30 paid Finance apps have ever reached the Top 25 best-selling apps. In contrast, nearly 2,300 game apps have cracked the top 25.

Revenue share from apps partners' in-app revenue holds much greater promise, however. For the opportunity to reach a much wider audience than they can on their own, apps developers should be very willing to strike deals with banks.

This will help banks expand and diversify their sources of revenue, expanding from a B2C business model to a B2B2C model.

Capitalizing on the finance mobile apps opportunity will require banks to significantly improve their marketing competencies, and, for many banks, it will mean developing new capabilities altogether.

PART V
THE NEW MARKETING

CHAPTER SEVENTEEN
MOBILE PAYMENTS:
THE FIFTH P OF MARKETING

How big are mobile payments? In late 2013, an article on BobsGuide.com, titled Mobile payments increased 19.5% on Cyber Monday, reported that:[81]

> "IBM said online sales during the day increased by 19% compared to 2012. However, retailers catering for mobile shoppers benefitted the most, seeing mobile traffic hitting 30 per cent of total site visits, a rise of more than 58% from last year. Since Thanksgiving, tablets have proved to be more popular for purchases, while mobile phones are preferred for browsing. Tablets accounted for 9.8% of purchases, compared with 5.7% from smartphones, IBM said. Consumers spent more cash when buying on tablets, with average order values hitting $128.30 per order, compared with $110.95 for smartphones."

Well, I'm confused. Did online sales grow by 19.5% or did mobile sales grow 19.5% from last year?

If it's the latter, I'm not impressed. The percentage of consumers who own a smartphone increased from about 38% in 2012 to roughly 60% in 2013. If mobile Cyber Monday sales only increased by 20%, that's not particularly impressive.

And I'm sure it was just a linguistic convention used by the author of the article, but exactly how did consumers use cash when making purchases from their tablets?

The bigger issue here is what constitutes a mobile payment. Does sitting at home, with a tablet on your lap, using a browser to surf the Web, and buying something constitute a mobile payment?

For that matter, if you're at home, and you use your smartphone to access a firm's website, and you buy something, should that count as a mobile purchase?

My take: Device shouldn't be the only factor determining what constitutes a mobile payment. Location matters.

When I'm sitting on the commuter rail train in Reading, MA, ready to head into Boston, and I access the MBTA app and buy my ticket before the conductor gets to me, that's a mobile payment.

When I access the Uber app on my smartphone from a bar in Atlanta to have a taxi come pick me up and take me back to my hotel, and the payment happens without an exchange of cash or swiping of credit or debit card, that's a mobile payment.

When I wave my smartphone in front of some device at Starbucks to pay for the lousy coffee they serve there, that's a mobile payment.

My own argument—that location matters—could come back to haunt me. If I imply that you have to be out-of-home in order for a payment to be considered a mobile payment, then wouldn't my making a purchase using a PC, accessing WiFi, while sitting at the airport, count as a mobile payment? I guess not, because it's the wrong device. What if I was using my iPad, instead of a PC, would that count?

Bottom line: As long as the numbers being reported include home-based, web-based purchases, I remain skeptical that mobile payment statistics really capture the shift in behavior.

The Path to Mobile Payments Adoption

In a Credit Union Times article, the author made the following assertion: Mobile banking adoption will drive mobile payment adoption. The idea was that banks should drive adoption of mobile banking among their customers in order to drive mobile payment adoption.

My take: Mobile shopping—not mobile banking—will drive mobile payments.

In the vast majority of countries, the adoption of online shopping (both purchasing and researching online) has historically outpaced—and continues to outpace—the adoption of online banking.

What did consumers do when the Internet started to take hold? They didn't start buying things right away, nor did they start managing their bank accounts online. They started by shopping—i.e., researching products and services.

As eCommerce opportunities expanded, consumers increasingly felt comfortable enough to buy online. The use of the channel to manage bank accounts quickly followed, but followed, nevertheless.

Bottom line: We'll see a similar—although much more time-condensed—pattern with mobile payments and mobile banking. In other words: Mobile banking doesn't drive mobile payments. Mobile shopping will drive mobile payments, which in turn will drive mobile banking. The flow will be: 1) Am I getting the best price? If yes, then...2) Do I have enough money (in checking account or on credit limit)? If yes, then... 3) Buy it.

Fat cats (like me), who don't worry about account balances, might check their account balance after a purchase. But, in any case, mobile banking adoption isn't going to drive mobile payment adoption.

Mobile shopping—comparing prices, researching product features, reviewing product reviews, and finding or accessing mobile coupons and merchant-funded offers--will be the stronger impetus to mobile payment adoption.

I'm not saying that mobile banking isn't important. Offering mobile banking capabilities is an imperative for banks because consumer demand is overwhelming and growing.

But banks must significantly improve their mobile marketing capabilities—in the form of cross-selling, influencing choice of payment cards, merchant-funded reward offers—in order to reap the benefits of mobile payment adoption.

Speed Bumps on the Path to Mobile Payment Disruption

Will mobile payments be disruptive? Depends on how you define it. If you think it means "put banks out of business" or "steal significant share of market away from banks," then, no, mobile payments will not be disruptive. I know the Disruptophiles disagree, but there are a number of speed bumps on the path to disruption that will keep banks in place for a long time:

1. **Scalability.** Scaling up some new payments technologies that rely on new physical devices—e.g., dongles, readers, beacons, etc.—will slow the growth in mobile payments. Scalability isn't just an issue on the merchant/retailer side—it's an issue for consumers as well, who are being asked to use key fobs, new devices, consolidate their cards on a single card, etc. In the long-run, this might not be the biggest speed bump out there, but anything that slows down the adoption of a new technology (or system) means the disruptors are burning cash.

2. **Privacy/security concerns.** There are a number of studies conducted recently that point to consumers' renewed interest in using cash, in response to the spate of breaches. I honestly can't see this as anything more than a blip, but

the privacy issues regarding the use of consumer data will rear its ugly heads. For every payment disruptor geek out there, there are two privacy fanatics who will make sure we all know that every step we take in a store is being tracked and monitored. The press loves these kind of stories more than stories about new methods of payment.

3. **Data management issues.** Remember when the financial services industry thought that account aggregation technology would give us insight into what the customer had, and was doing, and would give us the ability to analyze that data, and make relevant offers, and deepen relationships, and drive up profitability, and enable us to all retire at 40? You think merchants, retailers, and the new technology startups trying to disrupt the payments industry are all that better at managing and using data? I've said it before, will say it again: Apple's Achilles' heel is its inability to manage and analyze data.

4. **Offer fatigue.** But let's say a few firms emerge that are really good at data management and utilization (Google it–I think you'll find one). What are they going to do with that data? They're going to inundate us with more marketing offers. They have to–that's their business model. The whole push to payments disruption is about eliminating interchange and lowering transaction costs. How will the disruptors make money if not by pushing offers at us, and showing merchants/retailers they're driving business to them? This is a shaky business model.

5. **Customer service.** Think back to the last time you had a problem with an online or mobile search you did, and had to contact Google's customer service department. How did that go? It didn't. They don't have a customer service department. Retailers and merchants who call Square for customer support hear a recorded message telling them to

go online. That don't cut it, folks. Here's Shevlin's Law Of Customer Service: The company that makes the money on a transaction has to provide the customer support. If I'm taking 10 cents on a transaction, and you're getting a dollar, and the customer has a problem–YOU provide the support, buddy. The inability for some disruptors to build and scale customer support services will bring 'em down. It's not as easy as just outsourcing it to India.

6. **Funding source.** With all this talk of payments disruption, there's something I just don't understand. Seriously, I just don't get it. If, when a consumer uses an alternative, or let's call it a disruptive, payment method, if the money has to come out of a traditional bank, is the traditional bank really being disrupted? True payments disruption isn't going to happen–as far as I'm concerned–until we change how and where we deposit our paychecks.

7. **Declining margins.** Every other industry in modern history has seen a decline in transaction processing costs as volume increases and technology improves. Except payments. The oligopolies and regulatory environment has propped up those costs for a long time. On one hand, pulling away those props is a boon for disruption. On the other hand, declining margins in payment processing means fewer potential disruptors will reach the scale necessary to profit from slim margins.

8. **Consumer demand.** Some of you disruptive payments geeks are deluded. You think everyone–let alone everyone your age–wants to use new, alternative, and disruptive payment methods. Far from it. Most people couldn't care less. Even a lot of Gen Yers. Not saying that demand won't be there in 10, or even five, years. But it's not here today–and that's yet another speed bump on the path to disruption.

9. **Regulatory direction.** The regulatory direction is a total wildcard impacting the path to payments disruption. The head of the Consumer Financial Protection Board has already signaled that his organization will be taking a look at new payment schemes. Although the CFPB's actions are generally more favorable to startups than the large banks, any regulatory action is bound to create costs (not the least of which will be compliance-related) that challengers will need to incur.

The Fifth P of Marketing

Students of marketing might remember the 4 Ps of marketing—product, place, price, and promotion. The concept (which, I think, originated with a Northwestern University marketing professor) describes four "levers" that marketers work with, adjust, or alter, in order to influence marketing results.

In the past few years, there have been numerous articles proclaiming the death of the 4 Ps. These assertions, however, have failed to disprove that product, place, price and promotion are no longer relevant. For sure, service and service-related factors like information regarding product usage has become important, but these factors simply expand our definition of product. Place used to mean the store, but again, with the advent of the Web, and now mobile, channels, the definition of place is simply expanded.

Bloggers and social media gurus try to add a 5th P to the mix. Articles claim that people, personality, personalization, and productivity are all the new 5th P. One article even said that the new 5th P of marketing was Peter (can you guess the name of the author?).

None of these proposed elements are valid because they're either an element of the existing 4Ps (e.g., packaging and personalization are really about the product) or they're simply not a lever (personality? really?) that can be managed by marketers to influence marketing results.

My take: The adoption of mobile payments will elevate Payments to become the 5th P of marketing.

On one hand, payments could be seen as simply an element of price. Incentivizing (not a real word, but go with me on this one) a customer to pay cash instead of credit because it's beneficial to the marketer could just be price manipulation.

But there's growing evidence that the choice of payment methods available for a particular product can influence a customer's choice of product—regardless of the price. And this would qualify payments as a lever—or 5th P—that marketers can manage.

This is old news for the auto industry. Auto manufacturers have made Payments (e.g., leasing vs. financing) a part of the marketing mix for a while now. In this case, I would argue that Payment is not an element of price. In fact, I'd bet most car buyers don't even realize exactly what price they're really paying when they accept a lease or financing offer for $250 per month for 24 or 48 months.

For other industries, however, the choice of payment methods is just beginning to influence choice of providers. Having processed some 42 million mobile payment transactions between January 2011 and Q2 2012, there's a strong case to be made that Starbucks has engendered customer loyalty through its mobile payment capabilities. Offering prepaid debit cards has also helped to keep Starbucks' customers loyal to the company.

Both of these capabilities—mobile payments and prepaid cards—are examples of how payments have influenced marketing results without changing the product, price, place, or promotion mix.

The original concept behind the 4Ps was that the elements were part of a marketing mix—and that marketers had to allocate resources between the elements of the mix to influence marketing results. Payments meets this criteria, especially in a retail context. In *It's The End of POS as We Know It*, Joe Skorupa writes:[82]

> "Though the benefits of having a mobile POS is surely directed towards improving customer service, it also frees up store space occupied by cash registers, typically in the range of 30–40 % of the total numbers on weekdays. This space can be effectively used to display/sell merchandise."

Bottom line: When the 4Ps of marketing were first conceived, the choice of payment methods were limited. Today, there are more payment methods available, and the list is growing. And because of the importance of technology to many people, the choice of payment methods available for a growing number of products makes Payment a legitimate element in the marketing mix. In other words, there's a new 5th P to marketing.

Chapter Eighteen
The New Bank Marketing

Over the past few years, we've seen a near obsession among bank (and to a lesser extent credit union) execs who borrow from the retailer playbook (i.e., Starbucks), and turn their branches into places where consumers can hang out, sit in comfy chairs, drink coffee, and get Wi-Fi access on their computers.

It hasn't worked. In trying to understand why, I figured out what's missing: Sex.

Not long ago, fast food chain Carl's Jr. launched a series of ads featuring Kim Kardashian, who, I'm told, is a rather sexy reality TV star. Apparently, the ads were somewhat on the erotic side. This wasn't the first time that Carl Jr. has used sex to sell his food. A few years ago, I remember ~~seeing~~ hearing about Paris Hilton slithering around in a Carl Jr.'s ad wearing very little.

According to a creative director at the ad agency that did the new spots, "guys love Kim and women really like her because she's a real woman with curves." Carl Jr.'s logic must be that running sexy ads will make people think one of three things: 1) If I eat Carl Jr.'s food I'll be sexy like Kim; 2) If I eat Carl Jr.'s food I'll get someone sexy like Kim; or 3) If I eat Carl Jr.'s food I'll see someone sexy like Kim at the restaurant.

So, my banker friends, if you're going to pursue this "we want a great retail-like experience at the branch," you're going to have start running sexy ads.

Here's what I was thinking: How about an ad with Giselle Whats-her-last-name (Brady?) pulling a checkbook out of her push-up bra?

Oh wait, that wouldn't work because no one has checkbooks any more.

Ok, then, how about Rikki and Vikki from A Double Shot at Love with the Ikki Twins transferring balances from their savings account to checking account on their iPhones while wearing sexy lingerie? (I had to Google "reality TV stars" to come up with this, you know).

Hold on, this isn't going to work either. Women manage the finances in the majority of the households in this country, so maybe banks need ads with hot studly-looking guys. But that logic is faulty, too, since the ad agency dude implied that as long as the woman used in the ad is a "real woman with curves", it would appeal to women as well as to men.

I guess I should leave the creative part to the experts in the advertising business. Clearly, they know what they're doing here. But what I do know is that it's time banks made banking sexy.

Seriously, though, banks have a challenge—banking isn't cool.

When Apple announces a new product, or even a new version of its iPhone, hundreds of people line up at Apple stores to be among the first consumers to get the product. Good luck finding anyone who would line up at a bank when it announces an upgrade to a checking account.

But wait. Is the problem that banking isn't cool, or that banks, themselves, aren't cool?

Coin and the TechCrunch Effect

Coin, launched in late 2013, is a programmable mag-stripe card that holds up to eight card details at a time, accessible via a button and miniature LED screen on the card.

I would have thought that an announcement involving mag-stripe technology would be sleep-inducing. I was wrong. According to NetBanker:[83]

> "In the week since Coin was announced, the 105-second demo video has racked up more than 6 million views, 26,000 likes, and almost 9,000 comments. The company said its original $50,000 crowdfunding goal was hit in 47 minutes."

Wow. Why the excitement? Well, NetBanker does go on to quote someone posting on Quora, who listed five reasons for the response:

> "1) The product solves a real problem, too many cards in the wallet; 2) Coin implies there is a limited supply; 3) It was selling for a limited time at 50% off; 4) It appealed to early adopters with a blend of "old" meets "new"; and 5) $5 referral credit (against the $50 cost) with a built-in sharing button at the end of the purchase process."

My take: Sorry, but these reasons don't cut it. Plenty of new products meet criteria 2 thru 5. Anybody can "imply" a limited supply, sell that limited supply for 50% off, and offer a referral fee. That can't be the reason for the "success."

So Coin's success must be because "the product solves a real problem, too many cards in the wallet."

Hate to disappoint you, but that doesn't survive scrutiny. Yes, it's true that many people have multiple payment cards in their wallet. But as a (more or less typical) guy, it isn't just payment cards I have in my wallet. I have my driver's license, my health insurance card, and my building ID card. Going from six cards to three or four cards isn't really solving the "problem."

If my wife is in any way typical, going from three or four payment cards to one does absolutely nothing to solve the "problem" of carrying all the things she carries around in her bag (which is nothing more than an incredibly over-priced leather "black hole" with a fancy logo on it).

Coin's initial "success" has little to do with rational, logical reasons like solving a "problem," referral fees, or appealing to early adopters with a blend of "old" and "new."

Coin's initial "success" is due to the TechCrunch Effect. That's it, folks. The one—and only—reason for Coin's "success" was coverage on TechCrunch.

With coverage from TechCrunch upon its pre-launch, Coin was perceived as "cool." And apparently, there are people out there who want to be perceived as "cool" themselves by associating with "cool" products.

Please note that these aren't "early adopters." In fact, I'd bet that many of these people stop using the product shortly after its release next summer. Once everyone can get their hands on it, it will cease to be cool. And that will ruin it for the pre-release buyers.

Personally, I'm not very bullish on the product. Not only do I think there's no real problem the product is addressing, the price point is another nail in the coffin.

When banks discontinued free checking and implemented a US$5 monthly charge, people revolted. How dare they charge me to use my own money! How dare they charge me for the convenience and security of writing checks, paying with a debit card, and taking money out of ATMs at 3:00 in the morning!

Coin wants US$100 for the "convenience" of storing multiple card information on a single card. Yet, we don't hear anybody yelling "How dare they charge me to use the cards I'm already using!"

(**Note:** Don't try to convince me that this convenience is worth US$100, but the convenience of a checking account with ATM access and debit card usage isn't worth US$60 per year.)

The marketing lesson here is the TechCrunch Effect. Creating "cool" creates awareness, and even demand.

If Coin had pre-launched at a financial services industry conference, we would have heard crickets. Creating cool within the banking industry isn't the same as creating cool among TechCrunchies.

Had a bank been the first to launch something like Coin, I can just imagine the reaction. There's no way TechCrunch (or any other techie publication, like Mashable) would have written about it, with its general anti-bank stance. The product would be seen as an evil attempt on the part of an evil bank to capture more of a consumer's payment data, in an evil effort to sell that data to other parties.

But as a start-up, Coin gets press in TechCrunch, gets the cool factor, and goes on to sell $50k worth of its product in 47 minutes.

TechCrunch wrote that Coin's selling out its US$50k pre-launch goal was "a testament to the desire for folks to leave their plastic at home."

Nonsense. It's a testament to the TechCrunch Effect.

What Marketing Needs To Do Better

Existing banks aren't going to benefit from the TechCrunch Effect. But there are goals bank marketers can strive for to improve the public's perceptions of banks:

1. **Have conversations.** The popularity of social media has helped to highlight one of marketing's big shortcomings: Marketing doesn't know how to have a conversation with a customer. News of the latest deals or new branch/store openings aren't part of the "conversations" I typically have, are they part of yours? Reality is that marketing doesn't

really know how to have conversations with customers and prospects, because they've never done it before. Marketers must learn how to have a conversation instead of just talking about how important conversations are.

2. **Become a magnet.** Targeting and prospecting are marketing tactics akin to finding needles in haystacks. They characterize the old world of marketing: Go out and find people who might become customers, hit them upside the head with the "right message at the right time" and drag them back to your cave and sell them more stuff. Rather than spending its time hunting to find people who might want to become customers, marketing should help make the firm a magnet that draws people in. I'm not saying that marketers should stop targeting and prospecting—I'm saying that there's something else it needs to do.

3. **Learn to sense-and-respond.** Social media listening platforms have evolved, but marketers still need to have the ability to use them effectively: Specifically, the ability to sense where a customer or prospect is in the customer lifecycle, and how to respond with the most appropriate offer, message, or guidance. Simply recognizing that the most appropriate response to a customer/prospect isn't an offer would be a major step for many firms. Marketing has focused on "inbound marketing" over the past few years, but so much of that focus has simply been linking outbound marketing efforts to inbound contacts. A good step, but not enough.

There are marketers who will read this, scoff, and think "marketing needs to grow the business and improve the return on its marketing dollars." Sorry for the sports analogy, but that's like the head coach of a sports team saying "we need to win more games." That's not what they need to do—that's the desired outcome.

It's not sexy, but marketing needs to start thinking (and doing) more about its competencies, capabilities, and processes.

Sense-and-Respond Marketing

Gary Hamel was the first management thinker to write about the concept of core competencies. It's too bad this concept has fallen out of favor.

For all the talk about new marketing approaches like search engine optimization, social networking, and the like, few marketing execs can really (let alone honestly) answer the question: What is my marketing department really good at—that is, what are its core competencies?

I often (half) jokingly say that most bank marketers have perfected three Ps of marketing: 1) **Predicting** what people will buy; 2) **Pushing** a bunch of marketing messages out to those customers/prospects; and 3) **Praying** for a better response and conversion rate than the last campaign.

The emergence of new marketing pressures (like SEO and social networking) will require marketers to not simply understand and utilize these new vehicles. The changing behaviors and attitudes of consumers will require that marketers develop a new core competency. I call this competency sense-and-respond marketing:

> "The ability to sense consumer needs and intentions based on their behaviors and actions, and to respond with appropriate advice, guidance, and offers."

When addressing the core competency question, marketing execs should assess how well their marketing department can:

- Sense where a customer is in the buying cycle based on the clues that they provide through in-person, call center, and online interactions;

- Alter the sequence, quantity, and content of messages based on those clues; and

- Respond within an appropriate timeframe (this does not always have to be "real-time") and through the appropriate channels.

The predictive ability that many firms have developed over the past 20 or so years will support them going forward. But the nature of this ability changes from simply predicting product need to predicting "message" need (awareness message, advice message, sales message).

Successful salespeople have a sense-and-respond capability. They look and listen to their prospect and then respond and guide the prospect through the steps of the buying process.

This is marketing's new competency requirement: Improving its ability to move customers through the buying cycle with a sense-and-respond capability. But many bank marketers fail to see that there are (at least) two sides of the coin here: sense and respond.

It's great if a bank can analyze its customers' spending habits, identify trends, and predict what those customers will buy. But without the ability to reach those customers with an offer—in a timely manner, and in a channel where they'll actually see the message—the analytics (or "sensing") is akin to a tree that falls in the forest where there's nobody around to hear it. Did it make noise? Who cares? It doesn't matter.

Many analytics vendors miss the boat here. They're so focused on doing the analysis and creating the models, that they fail to recognize that banks wrestle with how to develop a new—and sustainable—marketing competency.

Many banks would love to improve their use of customer data to make better marketing and business decisions. But they don't want to simply do one-off projects that create and execute a single campaign. And they don't want to simply deploy some technology solution. The technology solution might be great at supporting an analytics function and process, but for most of these mid-sized banks, there is no function or process.

Tom Davenport is the author of *Competing on Analytics* and a leading light in a number of management innovations over the past 20 years. I first heard of Tom in the early 1990s when he wrote a Harvard Business Review article about business process redesign. He later wrote about knowledge management, and now champions the use of analytics for management decision-making.

Davenport believes that we're in a "new quantitative" era. Businesses need new decision approaches, that will be driven by enterprise analytics (which are comprised by web analytics, marketing analytics, supply chain/operations research analytics, human resources analytics, predictive analytics, etc.). As he said at a Web Analytics conference, "analytics without plans for decision-making is a waste of time."

My take: Analytics professionals need to fix problems—not just identify them. They need to tell a story with data, help frame decisions, and stand firm when necessary.

At the analytics, conference, Davenport displayed a chart that purported to show the relationship between competitive advantage and analytical maturity (other citations I've seen of this model label the X axis as "degree of intelligence") (Figure 18.1).[84]

Figure 18.1

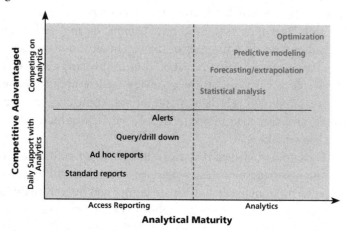

Source: Tom Davenport

My take: This model isn't correct. It ignores the respond side of the sense-and-respond coin.

Davenport's model is wrong because it ignores the respond side of the sense-and-respond construct. Simply developing optimization or predictive models does not make you a mature marketer if you haven't figured out how to take the output of those models and respond effectively and in a timely manner.

Analytical maturity isn't a function of how "intelligent" a company's analytical approaches and models are. It's a function of:

1. **Alignment.** Specifically, the alignment of analytical approach with the type of decision that needs to be made or the issue or problem that the firm is facing. Not every business problem requires an optimization or predictive model. Would you want to take a less-than-intelligent approach to solving a business problem? Of course not. That's why drill-downs and alerts are not less intelligent

than a predictive model. It all depends on what problem is being addressed.

2. **Sense-and-respond ability.** Queries, drill downs, and alerts might not be high on Davenport's intelligence scale. But they can often be accomplished more quickly than a firm can develop, test, and implement a predictive or optimization model. Often, it's the fastest response that wins, not the most elegant.

   When I first began thinking about the sense-and-respond construct, I thought there was a third component: Assessment. I thought "first we sense, then we respond, then we evaluate or assess our actions." But upon further thought, I realized that wasn't quite right. Assessment/evaluation is just another form of sensing. It's a continuous loop—we sense, respond, sense, respond, etc. So a contributor to how mature your analytics capability is depends not just on whether you respond in a timely fashion, but how well you assess how effective your analytics are, and can recalibrate and adjust your models and approaches.

3. **Data usability.** In the list of factors determining analytical maturity, this is certainly not the last one that should be mentioned, but the immature use of data often stems from a cultural immaturity. As I mentioned above, plenty of firms have developed predictive and optimization models to drive their marketing efforts. But many still use a relatively narrow set of data to power those models. Specifically, they often do not incorporate web-based data. An analytically mature marketing department uses a range of data sources, and gathers data for their analytical efforts more effectively and efficiently than a less-mature firm.

Bottom line: There is an analytics skills gap in banks. The gap is that highly sophisticated statistical approaches are deployed, but often in a very untimely manner and with a limited set of data. On the other hand, while web analytics efforts are often more timely, and incorporate a more efficiently gathered set of data, these efforts haven't grown beyond relatively simplistic analytic approaches.

Activity-Based Marketing

The adoption and assimilation of mobile devices into consumers' everyday activities, will lead to the emergence of another new marketing competency banks will need to develop: Activity-based marketing:

> *Marketing within the context of an activity being performed by a customer or prospect.*

A recent announcement by restaurant chain Chili's regarding tabletop computer screens is a great example of activity-based marketing: The activity is the process of ordering food.

At its most basic level, asking "would you like fries with that?" is a form of activity-based marketing. You might think of it simply as up-sell or cross-sell—and I would agree—but it doesn't quite seem like marketing because no principles of marketing (targeting, segmentation, promotion) are applied.

But they could be applied.

That's the potential of these tabletop computer screens. Not that they just simplify the ordering process. But that they push (i.e., merchandise) certain entrees, track your visits and tell you what you ordered last time, connect you with other diners to see what they like, etc. This technology shouldn't just streamline the ordering activity — it should transform it.

A narrow-minded banker might think "we already have things like this—ATMs and video tellers."

Wrong. Those deal with service transactions and interactions. These aren't the "activities" I'm talking about. I'm talking about activities like car-buying, house-shopping, and ticket-purchasing, or even shopping for more mundane items like shoes (that was a joke, guys, the ladies—at least the ones in my family—hardly consider shoes to be "mundane").

There are a number of examples of financial institutions already doing activity-based marketing:

1. **USAA.** USAA's Auto Circle app changes the car buying process by providing car shoppers with an app that lets them search for the type of car they want, track those cars for future reference and comparison, get a loan for the car when they're ready to buy it, and insure it as well. Transformation of the car-buying activity or process (Figure 18.2).

Figure 18.2

Source: USAA

2. **Commonwealth Bank.** This Australian bank's app uses augmented reality technology to let customers "take a picture" of a home or building, determine the location, access the realtor database, and display the price and details of the home if it's for sale. The app enables Commonwealth to identify potential mortgage customers long before it was able to do so in the past.

I don't know if Commonwealth is doing this or not, but the app could give other marketers—those interested in reaching new movers (who typically spend thousands of dollars in the six months after moving)—an opportunity to reach prospects even before they move, enabling Commonwealth to generate advertising revenue (Figure 18.3).

Figure 18.3

Source: Commonwealth Bank

3. **Caixa Bank.** Caixa Bank in Spain has developed an app that enables consumers to buy tickets (movies, sports, etc.) using their mobile device. It transforms the ticket-buying activity, and gives Caixa Bank the opportunity to steer payments to the method preferable to the institution, In addition, it gives the bank access to information about its customers that can help the bank generate advertising revenue from other marketers (Figure 18.4).

Figure 18.4

Source: CaixaBank

A common thread in the examples above is the creation of a new point of interaction for banks. Historically, banks' point of interaction with customers or prospects is the point of purchase—when the consumer is ready to buy the house

257

and needs to find a loan, or when the consumer is sitting down with the car dealer negotiating price.

For a host of other types of purchases, banks' point of interaction doesn't occur until consumers swipe their debit or credit card, or—even worse—after the transaction itself, when the check clears.

Activity-based marketing changes the point of interaction for banks, moving that point much closer to the identification of the need or want for the product or service (Figure 18.5).

Figure 18.5

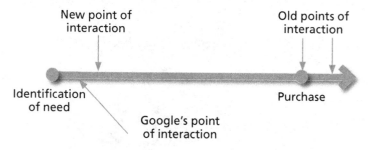

New point of
interaction

Old points of
interaction

Identification
of need

Google's point
of interaction

Purchase

Source: Author

Moving that point of interaction gives banks opportunities to influence the choice of providers. But it does so in a way that provides value to the consumer by transforming the overall activity.

Want to know why Google is worth gazillions? Because its point of interaction is so close to the consumer's identification of the need or want for a product. Brett King was spot-on when he wrote, in a post title *When Payments Disappear, and Value Emerges:*[85]

"Arguing over whether a payment is truly mobile or something else is a lost argument. When a payment ultimately works, no one is going to care how it happened. As long as it happened seamlessly with minimum fuss, and maximum context or value. When the payment disappears, it doesn't matter how you paid, it matters what the payment did for you."

This demonstrates the narrow-mindedness of too many bankers. Namely, those worried about what channel the order is taken in. So what if the mortgage application is taken online or in the branch? It doesn't matter—as long as your bank gets the application. And how does a bank ensure that it gets the application? By getting involved in the shopping process as early as possible.

The challenge is: How do banks get value to emerge? The answer is activity-based marketing.

Marketing is the New Customer Service

If I had a nickel for every time a credit union executive said his or her credit union's competitive advantage was its superior service, I wouldn't have to work for a living.

There are a number of issues with this claim, not the least of which is the nebulous way in which service is defined and the lack of quantitative measurement to support the claims (you provide better service? how much better?). New research supplies another angle to the argument. According to Zendesk:[86]

"As many as 67% of consumers prefer helping themselves to speaking with a customer service agent. An overwhelming 91% also said they would use a company's knowledge base if it was available and tailored to meet their needs."

In other words, NO service is the best service. Zendesk reports something they call the Self-Service Score, the number of users that attempt to use content made available by a company to solve an issue divided by the number of users that submit a request for an answer. The company computes the average score across industries at 4.1, which means "that for every four customers that attempted to solve their own issues via self-service, one customer chose to submit a support request." As the report goes on to state:[87]

> "Technical industries and manufacturers are leaders in this space, as they have had the most success with self-service, while industries like travel and financial services are having the least."

So, credit unions, tell me again why your service is so great?

The root of the issue is the nebulous definition of service. Exactly what constitutes "service"? The legacy view of service is tied to face-to-face or person-to-person interactions in which a customer has a question or problem, and the company's representative answers the question or resolves the issue.

Well, there's a helluva competitive advantage: "We fix our mistakes faster and friendlier than the other guy."

And, anyway, a data point from Zendesk's research shows that post-purchase service is the most important factor influencing loyalty for a lower percentage of consumers than the percentage that consider the purchase experience to be the most important factor. Nearly half said the most critical time to gain loyalty is when they make the first purchase.

So, are credit unions' sales/purchase/application processes really that much better than the big banks' process? One source says they're not. A study conducted by RateWatch and IntelliShop found that:[88]

"Credit unions, for all their benefits, just aren't as good as big banks at closing the deal with prospective customers."

The study, which was based on mystery shopping, not consumer surveys, found that big banks (>$10B assets) are better than credit unions when it came to:

- **First impressions.** Mystery shoppers entering large banks were immediately greeted by a customer service rep 76% of the time, compared to 53% of the time at credit unions.

- **Asking the right questions.** Mystery shoppers went in prepped to answer 11 anticipated questions. According to the article, "the large banks were much more consistent than the smaller institutions at asking the right questions to determine a prospective customer's needs."

- **Building confidence.** Forty-two percent of mystery shoppers left the big banks feeling "confident that this bank would be the right choice," compared to just 30% who said the same of the credit unions and 22% at the small banks.

Putting the two pieces of this puzzle together yields this: If self-service is the best service, and the most critical time for gaining loyalty is the initial purchase experience… then if you don't have the best online (i.e., self-service, self-directed) application processes in place, you don't have the best service.

But hold on a second here. Before you rush out to invest millions in online account opening technology…

Aite Group's research on banks' digital marketing maturity shows that online account creation capabilities exceed demand generation and demand conversion capabilities. Why is this a problem? If you don't fill the digital pipeline, having online account opening capabilities aren't optimized.

Let's add a third component to this:

1) The best service is self- (i.e., no) service.

2) If you don't have the best online application processes in place, then you don't have the best service.

3) If you don't have good digital marketing (i.e. demand generation and demand conversion) capabilities, you can't optimize your online account creation capabilities.

Bottom line: You know those misguided people who say that customer service is the new marketing? They're wrong! Marketing is the new customer service!

OK, so maybe marketing isn't the new service. But claims of superior service by credit unions aren't just unsupportable, they're unproductive in helping banks figure out where to invest and what capabilities they must create and improve.

Forget The Sales Culture

A lot has been written about the need for banks to create a "sales culture." There's even a site called creditunionsalesculture.com, run by a consulting firm.

There's a reference on the site to a survey which found that 75% of fast-growing credit unions had "installed" a sales culture, leading the authors of the study to conclude that "if you do not have a service selling culture—get one." Like it's that easy (and the reference to "installing" a sales culture is misguided—you install a washing machine or a refrigerator, you don't install a sales culture).

The problem with a lot of the discussion regarding a sales culture is that little of it revolves around what it is, and too much of it are just assertions that it's what banks need. How can you know you need it if you don't what it is?

A creditunions.com article titled *Four Critical Steps in Building a Successful Sales Culture* recommends: 1) Assessing and selecting any new staff in four critical sales culture dimensions prior to hiring; 2) Implementing an internal/external customer service program; 3) Teaching the staff the proper way to sell and self-promote; and 4) Coaching everyone.[89]

If you successfully did these four things, would your business performance improve? Without data about your customers' or members' preferences, needs, goals/objectives, etc., the Four Steps—in and of themselves—won't guarantee success. You still need a process that tracks, monitors, measures, and enforces when sales discussions are conducted with customers.

So is a sales culture really a prerequisite to success? Sales training expert Tim Wackel says no:[90]

> "Quit trying to sell. The less you worry about the sell the more you'll sell. Quit acting like a seller and act like a buyer—the world will pay more attention to you if you do. Don't communicate 'I'm here to sell you something.' Instead listen with them, dialogue with them and help them."

Sounds like the antithesis of a sales culture to me. Credit union CEO Gene Blishen, commenting on a blog post about sales cultures on Filene Research Institute's website, wrote:

> "Larger credit unions have moved to a sales culture. The staff needs to make the sales benchmarks set by management. The culture of service, though voiced admirably, is mostly just lip service. You can't have both. I asked a retiring CEO if he could do anything over again, what would it be. He said he would have never introduced a sales culture, it destroyed his credit union. They are big now, but at what price?"

There will always be studies where someone identifies the "high performers" and finds that 75% of them say they have a sales culture. But what we should be asking is how did the other 25% achieve high-performing status without one? And could the 75% who achieved high-performing status have done so without putting the time and effort into developing a sales culture?

It would be foolish to recommend that one-size-fits-all, and that every bank needs this or needs that. A sales culture may be exactly what some banks need. What I'm going to propose might not be the right thing for all banks, either. But it is appropriate for a lot of them.

My take: What banks need is an advice/guidance culture. A culture in which the organization is driven to provide the right advice, guidance, help, counsel, instruction, persuasion, dissuasion, suggestion, prescription, recommendations, and caution to its customers. Advice and guidance that helps customers maximize and optimize the performance of the financial accounts they have, and of their financial lives, in general. This change in focus (from sales to advice/guidance) does a few things for a bank. An advice/guidance culture:

- **Broadens the focus beyond human interactions.** One problem with a sales culture, as it's typically done in banks today, is that it is focused on human-to-human interactions (which are in decline, and are likely to continue to do so). But advice/guidance can be provided in any channel. Figuring out how to provide advice/guidance across channels (especially in the online and mobile channels) is a more important challenge for banks to address than developing a sales culture.

- **Takes the focus off of individual employee skills or capabilities.** Becoming a bank of 2020 means change, and people naturally resist change (even if they want it, and even if it's to their benefit). Changing the culture to a sales culture is a struggle for many bank employees, especially those with a distaste for "sales." Many bank employees resist building a sales culture because they don't believe they can develop sales skills, or don't want to. An advice/guidance culture, however, is less offensive, and focuses on organizational—not individual—skill sets.

- **Aligns more closely with the organization's mission.** Which of the following two statements is closest to your organization's mission? Is it a) To sell the most products to our customers or members. Or b) To best serve our customers' or members' financial services needs. You said b), didn't you? OK, now which kind of culture is best aligned with that mission? A sales culture or an advice/guidance culture? That's what I thought.

Bottom line: It's time to retire the notion that banks and credit unions need a sales culture to succeed. An advice/guidance culture is what banks need in order to compete on performance.

AFTERWORD:
FROM MONEY MOVEMENT TO
MONEY MANAGEMENT

In the annals of the Harvard Business Review, Marketing Myopia by former HBS professor Ted Levitt, is a classic. The article introduced the question:[91]

> "What business are you really in?" and with it the claim that, had railroad executives seen themselves as being in the transportation business rather than the railroad business, they would have continued to grow. The article is as much about strategy as it is about marketing, but it also introduced the most influential marketing idea of the past half-century: that businesses will do better in the end if they concentrate on meeting customers' needs rather than on selling products."

My take: This concept of myopia is a big problem facing banks today. The problem isn't about being "digital." It's about misunderstanding how the business is changing, what business they need to be in, and how the business model needs to adapt.

In a survey of credit union executives conducted by Aite Group and Filene Research, when asked about their new product and service initiatives for 2014, the overwhelming number of responses related to traditional products and services (i.e., checking accounts, credit cards, mortgages, car loans).

In other words, coming up with a new flavor of a checking account, or a variation on a mortgage or car loan is what many of these executives see as "new" or "innovative."

You would have a hard time convincing me that a survey of community bank execs would produce significantly different results. And while I do believe that the largest banks are exploring non-traditional opportunities, those innovation initiatives are like small cabins on huge ocean liners.

Yet, when I read blog posts and white papers, the focus seems to be on "becoming more digital" or "accelerating innovation." Becoming more digital, like offering mobile account opening is not a long-term strategy if the concept of an "account" is going to radically change (i.e, go away). And innovating without a clear idea of what the strategic goal is, it is kind of wasted effort, no?

The problem with banking execs is analogous to the problem the railroad execs, described in HBR's Marketing Myopia, had: How they define their business. Bank execs predominantly see banks as being in the "money movement" business. This explains the current obsession with mobile payments, and how the world of payments is changing. The pundits all yell and scream about how every new payments-related announcement is going to disintermediate banks and put them out to pasture, or cause them to become extinct.

Got news for you (and you won't agree this): Payments are a losing business (for banks).

A student of business history would understand this. In industry after industry, the ability for any company to sustain revenue growth from transaction processing is a losing proposition. Advances in technology continue to push the cost of transaction processing near zero, and in the absence of any added value to the processing of a transaction, companies can't sustain growth.

The current upheaval in the payments business isn't really about mobile technologies, it's about cost. As consumers' payment behavior shifted from cash and checks to cards (both credit and debit, but predominantly to debit), retailers' and merchants' transactions increased. The purported "value-add" was improved risk management and faster money movement, but retailers and merchants either don't see those benefits, or refuse to see those benefits.

So it's great that there are innovators coming along to change the world of payments. And it's hardly surprising that retailers and merchants would want to adopt payment mechanisms that will undercut the existing payment networks.

But what happens in 10 years if and when PayPal is the dominant payment network? Guess who the next target of change is? The bottom line here is clear: Making money off transactions–or as the banks see it, money movement–isn't a sustainable business model.

Just as railroad execs needed to see themselves in the transportation business, not the railroad business, bankers need to see themselves in the "money management" business, not the "money movement" business.

This is hard for bankers to see, or to accept, because–today, at least–there's no money to be made in the money management business. With monthly fees for just keeping a checking account open, and penalties for bad account behavior that could triple or quadruple the monthly fees, consumers simply aren't willing to pay for money management capabilities.

Furthermore, the money management capabilities that are offered today aren't worth paying for, as far as many consumers are concerned. Budgeting and expense categorization? Eh.

It may be hard to see today—on the heels of a downturn in the economy, and a predominance of Gen Yers without a lot of money to spend—but for the vast majority of consumers, improving the way they manage their money is the most pressing financial services-related challenge.

Borrowing money (the lending side of banks' business) is just one part of the money management problem. Consumers don't want to borrow money, they need to. Mark my words: You will always make more money by providing what consumers want than what they need. Sure, they'll pay for what they need, but will look to minimize that expense. Serving their desires, on the other hand...

And make no mistake about it. Despite the sorry state of the economy, we spend money like it's going out of style (oh wait, maybe it is). In the 20-year period from 1992 to 2012, real retail spending (seasonally adjusted) increased ~50%, completely recovering from the dip experienced during the recession.

With retail sales exploding, and the number of retail sales transactions with it, it's little surprise that retailers and merchants would rebel against transaction (i.e., interchange) fees.

The drivers of consumer change, however, usually fall into some combination of two categories: Cost and convenience. Although retailers and merchants pass interchange fees through to consumers, consumers don't perceive this very clearly. And the added convenience of mobile, or alternative, payment mechanisms is not clear to a lot of consumers.

Start-ups like Simple and Moven seem to get this. I say "seem" because sometimes I'm not sure if they see their differentiation as "mobile" or "money management." Mobile isn't a differentiator. It's simply an access or transaction channel. Ho hum.

But with features like Simple's "safe to spend" and Moven's real-time digital receipts and money tracking, the startups are showing the industry signs of what money management could look like. Mobile is simply the mechanism by which these features are delivered. The value, however, is in the feature, not the choice of device.

Banks have been given a lot of grief over the past few years for being slow, out of touch, whatever. Lots of pundits seem to think they'll disappear like the dinosaurs in the next few years.

I guess that view sells books and drives page views.

But I'm not nearly as pessimistic. Why? Because of the opportunity for banks to demonstrate customer advocacy (i.e., to be an advocate for the consumer, not that net promoter score, "get the consumer to advocate for us" nonsense).

Retailers and merchants offering mobile wallets to facilitate payments aren't doing so for the benefit of consumers. They're doing so to drive sales. Is a merchant or retailer really going to tell you its product or service isn't the best? Or that there's a better price somewhere else? Or that you can do better by using a payment mechanism that charges the retailer a higher interchange fee?

In addition, with data breaches announced practically every week, how long will it be before consumers lose confidence that retailers and merchants can be trusted with personal, confidential, or sensitive data?

Bottom line: The opportunity for banks (and, in particular, credit unions) to position themselves as customer advocates is huge. Unfortunately, so is the shift in mindset needed to move from seeing the business as "money movement" to "money management." It's this myopia that's slowing banks down—not the technology.

The path to success in banking isn't about moving money faster. It's about developing products and services that will help the next generation of bank customers better manage their (hopefully) growing amount of money–and that they will (more willingly) pay for these products and services.

Acknowledgements

There are a number of people who deserve credit (or blame, it's your call) for making this book a reality. In addition to writing the Foreword, Brett King's behind-the-scenes contributions to the book are too numerous to mention, and actually started years ago.

Back in 2012, Brett and I were having lunch in New York, and I (half-) joked that I was going to write a book, and knock him off the pedestal as the industry's leading conference speaker on bank innovation. Most people would respond by saying (or thinking) "bring it on, sucker!" Not Brett. His response was "how can I help?" And truth be told, the title of this book really came from Brett, too.

Thanks to Shari Storm, former Chief Marketing Officer of Verity Credit Union, and author of Motherhood is the New MBA for her contributions to the Moms: The Real Decision Makers which was based, in large part, on written and verbal conversations with Shari.

There is a group of people who regularly read and comment on my blog, Snarketing 2.0, and who deserve a lot of credit for shaping the content of this book: Bradley Leimer, Jim Marous, Alex Jimenez, Sam Maule, Deva Annamalai, Charles Potts, Cherian Abraham, Matt Wilcox, and Ketharaman Swaminathan.

Thanks also go out to Jeffry Pilcher, publisher of The Financial Brand, for all his support going back a number of years now.

I also want to give a special thanks to David Gerbino. When I started blogging in 2006, I had no idea what to expect. I had never even read a blog before I started writing one. The first subscriber to my blog was a former Forrester Research colleague of mine. The second subscriber was David Gerbino. Thanks for sticking with me all these years, David.

Last, and certainly not least, thanks to my publisher Ashwin Rattan, for persisting as long as he did to get me to do this, and make this whole thing possible.

References

1   Wall Street Journal, "Tally of U.S. Banks Sinks to Record Low," December 3, 2013.

2   Slate, "America's Microbank Problem," December 2, 2013.

3   The Federalist, "No, America Doesn't Have Too Many Banks," December 3, 2013.

4   http://en.wikipedia.org/wiki/The_Incredible_Shrinking_Man

5   Knowledge@Wharton, "The Shrinking U.S. Banking Sector: On Balance, Who Benefits?." April 27, 2011.

6   American Banker, "What Matthew Yglesias Should Have Said About Small Banks," December 11, 2013.

7   McKinsey Consulting, "The State of Global Banking—In Search of a Sustainable Model," September 2011.

8   Boston Consulting Group, "Distribution 2020: The Next Big Journey for Retail Banks," March 2013.

9   "The Evolution of Science-Based Business: Innovating How We Innovate," Oxford University Press, 2010.

10 Harvard Business Review, "Imitation Is More Valuable Than Innovation," April 1, 2010.

11 Knowledge@Wharton, "Why Disruptive Innovation Can Help Market Leaders," August 7, 2014.

12 Washington Post, "What Are Your Worth to Your Bank?," April 6, 2010.

13 Brett King, Bank 3.0: *Why Banking Is No Longer Somewhere You Go But Something You Do*, (Wiley, 2012).

14 ibid.

15   November 2009 Harvard Business School Club of New York presentation, quoted on TrustedAdvisor.com, http://trustedadvisor.com/trustmatters/trust-is-the-new-black-insights-from-craig-newmark-of-craigslist

16   MediaPost, "Trust Is a Beautiful Thing," November 19, 2009.

17   Glen Urban, "Trust-Based Marketing," MIT Sloan Working Paper No. 4302-03, March 2003.

18   The Financial Brand, " Measuring 'Trust' In Banking: A Misguided Metric," October 17, 2012.

19   Cited in MarketingCharts.com, "Americans Trust Soft Drink Advertising," February 15, 2010.

20   The Financial Brand, "This Bank's Brand Ads are Out of Control," November 18, 2008.

21   ABA Bank Marketing, "Welcome Aboard," December 2007.

22   Adweek, " WaMu Wants Customers Yelling 'Whoo Hoo!'," February 13, 2008.

23   Advertising Research Foundation, http://thearf.org/research-arf-initiatives-defining-engagement

24   Chief Marketer, " Seven Brand and Marketing Trends for 2007," November 10, 2006.

25   American Banker, " What Engagement Banking Needs Is Less Engagement," September 12, 2013.

26   Aite Group, "A Behavioral Segmentation of Banking Customers," April 2013.

27   Aite Group, "Strategies for FFM Success," September 2012.

28   Federal Reserve Bank of Cleveland, "Do Bank Branches Matter Anymore?," August 4, 2011.

29   Chris Skinner, *Digital Bank: Strategies to Launch or Become a Digital Bank*, (Marshall Cavendish International, 2014).

30   CNBC, "A New Era of Branch Wars at Nation's Big Banks," April 10, 2013.

31   American Banker, " Conestoga Takes Branch Video to the Next Level," June 29, 2012.

32   San Francisco Business Times, "Young Adults Say They Don't Trust Banks," September 30, 2009.

33   Aite Group, The Coming Credit Card Boomlet, June 2014.

34   LemmonTree Marketing Group, "Understanding the New Age Wave: Gen Y," http://www.lemmontree.com/PDF/Understanding_New_Age_Wave_Gen_Y.pdf

35   The Financial Brand, "Why Gen-Y Opens Accounts In Branches And Not Online," July 9, 2013.

36   "Read what happens when a bunch of over-30s find out how Millennials handle their money." quartz.com, http://qz.com/277509/read-what-happens-when-a-bunch-of-over-30s-find-out-how-millennials-handle-their-money/

37   CU Insight, "Getting Younger Important, But So is Staying Older." October 5, 2012.

38   Credit Unions Online, "The Credit Union World Attracting Gen Y to Ensure Its Bright Future," August 14, 2012.

39   Thrivent magazine, "Women: Face Your Financial Hurdles," Summer 2013.

40   Credit Union Times, " Marketing to Women Requires Cultural Change," February 26, 2012.

41   Holly Buchanan, "Marketing Credit Unions to Women," February 5, 2011, http://marketingtowomenonline.typepad.com/blog/2011/02/marketing-credit-unions-to-women.html

42   Email correspondence with the author.

43   MarketingCharts, "How Marketers Should Appeal to Women," March 22, 2010.

44   Payments Source, "Consumers Show Cautious Interest In Mobile Payments," March 23, 2012.

45   American Banker, "Reaching the Underbanked? Try Offering Control, Research Says," March 6, 2013.

46   Federal Deposit Insurance Corporation, National Survey of Unbanked and Underbanked Households, June 2011.

47   Knowledge@Wharton, "A Question of Value: Bringing Banks to the Unbanked," October 24, 2012.

48   New York Times, "Over a Million Are Denied Bank Accounts for Past Errors," July 30, 2013.

49   http://en.wikipedia.org/wiki/Disruptive_innovation

50   ibid.

51   American Banker, "Time to Face the Music On Disintermediation." February 1, 2012.

52   Aite Group, "Strategies for PFM Success," September 2012,

53   Filene Research, "The Future of Member-Facing Technologies in Credit Unions," 2010.

54   NetBanker, " Will Mobile Finally Make PFM Popular?," July 29, 2013.

55   Federal Reserve Bank of St. Louis, Economic Research, http://research.stlouisfed.org/fred2/series/RSXFS

56   Cicero, " Made in heaven or marriage from hell? Social media and the financial sector," 2012, http://www.cicero-group.com/wp-content/uploads/2012/01/Cicero_SoMe_Report_200112_Web.pdf

57   Aite Group, "Financial Advisors' Use of Social Media 2011: The Bloom Is Off the Rose," December 2011.

58   Social Media Today, "Can Financial Services and Social Media Co-Exist and Succeed?," January 8, 2013.

59   Harvard Business Review, "Why Your Social Media Metrics Are a Waste of Time," December 18, 2012.

60   IBM Institute for Business Value, "From Social Media to Social CRM," February 2011.

61   Business2Community, "5 Ways to Measure Social Media Success," March 25, 2012.

62   Mashable, "5 Best Practices for Financial Institutions on Facebook," October 24, 2011.

63   Snarketing 2.0, "Banks' Social Media Gender Challenge," July 9, 2012.

64   MediaPost, " Women Be Dominatin' Social Media," July 6, 2012.

65   http://www.collaborativefinance.org/rosca/

66   FutureLab, "3 Ways Retail Banks Could Get More Benefit from Social Media," February 23, 2012.

67   creditunions.com "Big Data at a Growing Credit Union," http://www.creditunions.com/articles/big-data-at-a-growing-credit-union/

68   Avanade, "Global Survey: Is Big Data Producing Big Returns?," June 2012, http://www.avanade.com/Documents/Research%20and%20Insights/avanade-big-data-executive-summary-2012.pdf

69   Originally found at http://www.enhanced-editions.com/blog/2012/02/book-promotion-analytics-and-a-new-marketing-approach-for-publishers/, link no longer available.

70   comScore, "Digital Wallet Road Map 2013," February 4, 2013.

71   Mobile Payments Today, "Report: Banks look to offers, data to own mobile payments," June 10, 2013.

72   American Banker, "Hold On, Convenience Just May Lead Consumers to Mobile-Pay," October 29, 2012.

73   Banking Technology, "Banks line up behind V.me by Visa digital wallet platform," November 30, 2102.

74   TechCrunch, "PayPal President David Marcus On Cyber Monday, In-Store Payments, Data Strategy And More," November 26, 2012.

75   Presentation at xxx conference by former Sprint CEO, Dan Hesse.

76   PR Web, "56% of Consumers Want to Have Deals Pushed to Their Smartphones According to BuyVia Survey," December 18, 2012.

77   Media Post, "78% Aware of Mobile Wallets, 32% Use Them," July 23, 2014.

78   Flurry Analytics, "Flurry Five-Year Report: It's an App World. The Web Just Lives in It," April 3, 2013.

79   Nielsen, " The State Of Mobile Apps,"

80   Canalys, "Top app stores risk losing control of app discovery," June 11, 2012.

81   Bob's Guide, "Mobile payments increased 19.5% on Cyber Monday," December 3, 2013.

82   Retail Info Systems News, "It's the End of POS as We Know It," http://risnews.edgl.com/retail-insight-blog/It-s-the-End-of-POS-as-We-Know-It81598

83   Net Banker, "Fintech Four from Last Week," November 25, 2013.

84   Thomas Davenport, *Competing on Analytics: The New Science of Winning*, (Harvard Business Review Press, March 2007).

85   Banking 4 Tomorrow, "When Payments Disappear, and Value Emerges," October 11, 2013.

86   Zendesk, "The Zendesk Benchmark Q2 2013," February 2013,

87   ibid.

88   Main Street, "Study: In Customer Service Battle, Big Banks Win," February 9, 2012, http://www.mainstreet.com/article/moneyinvesting/savings/study-customer-service-battle-big-banks-win?page=1

89   creditunions.com, "Four Critical Steps in Building a Successful Sales Culture," http://www.creditunions.com/articles/four-critical-steps-in-building-a-successful-sales-culture/

90   Quoted on http://blog.markarnold.org/2011/04/improving-your-credit-union-sales-culture.html

91   Harvard Business Review, "Marketing Myopia," July 2004, http://hbr.org/2004/07/marketing-myopia/ar/1

CPSIA information can be obtained
at www.ICGtesting.com
Printed in the USA
FSOW03n1506051016
25579FS